A Haven
from
HITLER

Heini Gruffudd

y Lolfa

The publishers wish to acknowledge the support of
Cyngor Llyfrau Cymru

Cover design: Robat Gruffudd

ISBN: 978 184771 817 4

Published and printed in Wales
on paper from well-maintained forests by
Y Lolfa Cyf., Talybont, Ceredigion SY24 5HE
website www.ylolfa.com
e-mail ylolfa@ylolfa.com
tel 01970 832 304
fax 832 782

Contents

Introduction

THIS IS A STORY of suffering and heroism, love and hatred, death and survival. It is the story of my mother, Kate Bosse-Griffiths and her family.

As a refugee from Nazi Germany she spent two years in Scotland and England before settling in Wales, firstly in the Rhondda Valley and then in Bala, and spent the remainder of her life in Swansea. She learnt Welsh and in a short period became an acclaimed Welsh-language author. Today the Egypt Centre at Swansea University is a testament to her interest in Egyptology.

Her story, and that of her family, is closely linked to the rise of Nazism in the 1930s and the Second World War.

Some families have suffered more than this one. In the carnage of the Second World War, large numbers of civilians as well as soldiers were victims of the killing. Jewish families in Germany and its occupied territories disappeared without trace, with no-one left to record their story.

This story involves a German family of Jewish descent and their attempts to stay alive. Different individuals responded to the difficulties of the time in different ways. Some took pride in their contribution to German life in an attempt to be accepted, or to avoid being persecuted, by the system. This did not mean agreement with the regime, but it did mean accepting the necessity of giving Caesar his due. Others attempted to deal with the challenge of carrying on in spite of the system, while the opposition of others to Nazism resulted in sacrifice and self-sacrifice. The threat of persecution hovered over them all.

The other strand of the story is Welsh, as my mother married into a Welsh-speaking family, whose members and friends cared for the future of their language and culture. Perhaps unwittingly, my mother created a literary circle that became known as 'Cylch Cadwgan'.

It is difficult to imagine how one of Europe's most civilized, cultured and creative countries became the world's most barbaric. By tracing anti-Semitism in Wittenberg where the Bosse family lived, one can see how circumstances evolved that welcomed a dictator. Few Germans themselves, nor Jews within the country, could have foreseen that this anti-Semitism would develop into a programme of systematic imprisonment and death.

What makes the telling of this story possible is that the family was a fairly literary one, and letters and family documents form the basis of the research. It is relevant to Wales because one member of the family found refuge here and became involved in our country's fate.

A thousand and more pages of the family's letters, documents and diaries have survived. A selection of them form the basis of this book. I have attempted to highlight the main events, and to portray the relevant background. Perhaps someone else would have chosen differently. This is the weakness of any history: the need to select. And although I have not set out to provide more interpretation than is relevant to the telling, the way the story is presented inevitably involves some personal views.

Documents such as these present a second difficulty, of course. One can be certain that they are not complete, and they are certainly not complete in the sense that they do not include the thoughts and actions of all involved at the time. A comment in a letter or diary can be a moment's fancy rather than a balanced and final consideration of a specific subject. There are comments here on people and on members of the family: it must be remembered that these are people's comments about each other, and we all know how our thoughts on others can change from hour to hour and year to year. May the host of witnesses forgive me if I have chosen material they would rather have left forgotten.

This, then, is a version of a story, but I hope that the main narrative is close to the truth, or as close to the truth as it can be as. The work is a memorial to a family that lived through the most difficult years of the twentieth century.

It was an honour that the original Welsh-language version of this book won the Welsh Book of the Year in 2013.

Heini Gruffudd
Abertawe
March 2014

Acknowledgements

M Y MOTHER HAD SPENT many years collecting and organising family papers, and Günther, her brother who lived in Sweden, had insisted that I visit him in Karlshamn to photocopy hundreds of documents, and to hear his story of survival. He did not want the story of his generation to be lost.

I received further information from other members of the family, including my cousin Ulrich, who now lives in Bielefeld, Westphalia, and my cousin Ute, who lives in Neckarhausen near Heidelberg. She and her husband Detlev have carried out detailed research through various family, church, town and army archives.

Robat, my brother, gave constant encouragement, and I was also encouraged by Gwennan Higham whose research degree was based on by mother's writing. I need to give particular thanks to Caryl Ebenezer, from the production company Rondo, who arranged a journey to Germany – to Berlin, Wittenberg and Ravensbrück – for me and my daughter Nona and her husband Matthew, and their children, Gwenllian and Greta, to investigate further the events associated with the Ravensbrück concentration camp. A programme of the journey was televised on S4C. I wish to thank Alun Jones of Y Lolfa press for his valuable suggestions on the content; Nia Peris, who assisted with detailed attention to the text in Welsh, and Eifion Jenkins and Eirian Jones for their work on the English version.

My other children, Efa, Anna and Gwydion, gave advice on earlier versions of the book and urged me to complete it so that the memory of a special generation is kept alive.

Some of the family's members

In Germany:

Paul Bosse – a surgeon, of German descent; my grandfather (often referred to in this material as Opa or Vati)

Kaethe Bosse – his wife, born Levin, of Jewish descent (the family changed its name to Ledien in 1914); my grandmother (often referred to in this material as Oma or Mutti)

Their children:

Dorothea (Dolly) Maier Bosse, their elder daughter

Kate (Käthe) Bosse-Griffiths, their second daughter; my mother

Günther Bosse, their elder son

Fritz Bosse, their second son

Other family members:

Hans Ledien, solicitor, brother of Kaethe Bosse

Erika Ledien (formerly Schulz), his wife

Erika (Ledien) Viezens, their daughter

Eva Borowietz, sister of Kaethe Bosse

Willibald Borowietz, army officer, her husband

Their children: Joachim, Wilma and Eva Monika

Kurt Ledien, second cousin of Kaethe Bosse

In Wales:

J. Gwyn Griffiths, academic, litterateur and nationalist, my father

FAMILY TREE OF KAETHE LEVIN (LEDIEN)
The main people mentioned in the book are noted in bold type.

Johanna Boas 1829–1901 = Adolph Levin 1826–1902

Max Levin 1856–1925 = Luise Hedwig Alexander 1863–1931

Louis Levin 1860–1922 = Gertrud Levin 1866–1965
Three children:

Suzanne Levin

Ulrich Levin 1895–1990

Kurt Ledien = Martha Liermann
1893–1945 1894–1978
Two children:
Ilse Ledien 1926–2002
Ulle Ledien 1929–

Eva Ledien = Wilibald Borowietz
1896–1938
Three children:
Joachim 1919–1940
Wilma 1922–
Eva Monika 1925–2006

Five children:

Käthe Ledien = Paul Bosse
1886–1944 1881–1947

Hans Ledien = Erika Schulz
1887–1963
One child:
Erika Ledien = Axel Viezens
1930–   1924–1979

Friedrich Ledien
1889–1916

Willy Levin
1892–1895

Fritz = Sophie Schnelle
1915–1965 1913–2008
Children:
Käthe 1946–
Ulrich 1952–

Four children:

Dorothea [Dolly] = Georg
1907–1993   1904–1986
Dolly's children:
Georg (Tippen) 1934–1971
Peter 1936–1940
Barbara 1938–
Eckhard 1941–
Roswitha 1942–2013
Ute 1944–

Kate = Gwyn Griffiths
1910–1998 1911–2004
Children:
Robat 1943–
Heini 1946–

Günther = Edith
1913–1999 1914–1976
Children:
Ingrid 1938– = (1) Justus
Kristina 1940–
Ingegerd 1948–
Polle 1955–

FAMILY TREE OF PAUL BOSSE

Johann Friedrich Bosse = Auguste Chatarine Memminger
1759–1807   1760–1817
|
Elias Friedrich Wilhelm Bosse = Maria Münch
1802–?   1805–1842
|
Julius Heinrich Wilhelm Bosse = Pauline Waymeyer
1838–1898   1851–1914
|

Paul Bosse	Kurt Bosse	Willi Bosse	Else Bosse	Ella Bosse
1881–1947	1878–?	1878–?	1884–1907	1872–1901

FAMILY TREE OF GWYN GRIFFITHS

In Rhosllannerchrugog: In Llansadwrn:
Ioan Griffiths = Jane Edwards   David Davies = Elizabeth Morgans
1852–1897   1855–?   1845–?   1850–?
| |
Robert Griffiths = Jemimah Davies
1876–1941   1884–1969
|

Elizabeth = Huw Jones	Augusta (Ogi)= Stephen Davies	Gwyn = Kate Bosse	David R. = Gladys	Gwilym = Edna Lewis
1905–1947 1907?–1947	1908–1991 1905–1960	1911–2004 1910–1998	1915–1990 ?–1982	1917–2002 1921–1996

PART 1

BACKGROUND

'Are you a Jew?'

I WAS COMING OUT OF Debenhams, in the Quadrant Shopping Centre in Swansea. A rabbi stood by the exit. For some reason he greeted me.

'Shalom!'

'Shalom,' I answered with a smile.

I'm not sure whether he was surprised by my answer, but I was certainly surprised by his question.

'Are you a Jew?'

How should I have answered? I was raised in Capel Gomer, a Welsh Baptist chapel, and I went to Sunday school at Trinity, a Welsh Methodist chapel. Now and again I went to a Unitarian chapel, and the memory of Amlyn, a dear college friend, the son of the Reverend Jacob Davies and an ardent Unitarian, who died after his first year at Aberystwyth, is still a matter of heartbreak to me. I then went to Tabernacl, Morriston, a Welsh Independent chapel, and now I am, of all things, a deacon at Bethel Sketty, again an Independent chapel. A Jew?

'I could be. My mother was of Jewish extraction.'

The rabbi's eyes brightened.

'Then you're a full Jew. You must come to the synagogue next Saturday.'

I smiled again, more timidly this time, but he soon obtained my phone number.

During the week I was called three or four times by the synagogue's elders, and I had no choice but to attend. I had a shawl to wear and a Jewish cap and took a seat with the faithful, while the women remained behind a wooden screen. There was chanting, reading from the scripture and a sermon, with a beaming rabbi proud of having found a prospective member.

'Watch yourself,' said one of the faithful. 'He'll make you a member if you're not careful. He's just here for a month or two – and he's being paid well!'

I was careful. But I followed the three-hour long service attentively. It was possible to understand the readings from a translated text, with explanatory notes emphasising the history of the Jews as a separate people. The members and the women conversed now and again, in sharp contrast to the respectable silence of our chapels.

One of the members was an old school friend of mine. I knew he was a Jew, and it was a pleasure to hear him taking part by singing one of the psalms. He told me afterwards, 'I'm not a believer, mind you, but we're keeping the tradition. If we keep it for another ten years, I will have played my part.' By now, ten years later, the synagogue has been sold to an evangelical church, but the Jewish congregation have kept a hall for worship.

Then came the ceremonial washing of hands before the meal that followed the service.

'The rabbi went to Birmingham to buy real kosher food,' I was told by a member of the congregation. And it was very tasty. But I had not prepared myself for the jokes – some of which were deliciously blue.

I left feeling honoured to have been part of the service, and that they had opened the door for me to join them. On one occasion my mother had presented this synagogue with a copy of a scroll of the book of Esther, a copy of an old manuscript that she had come across in her archaeological activities. But I also knew that simply being of Jewish descent was not enough for me

17

to belong to them. My tradition is a different one, and my Welsh father ensured that I grew up in the cauldron of Welsh culture. Jumping from one tradition to another is not possible without a long period of immersion.

My father's roots are in two counties: Carmarthenshire and Denbighshire. In Ponciau near Rhosllannerchrugog my grandfather, Robert Griffiths, was one of a dozen children. Others in the family made a considerable sacrifice to enable him and his brother to study for the ministry. His first chapel was Elim Parc, near Carmarthen, and he then went to Bethabara, near Eglwyswrw, Pembrokeshire, before putting down roots in Moreia chapel, Pentre, Rhondda. Jemimah Davies, my grandmother, was brought up in the Llansadwrn area, and in Talyllychau church graveyard my ancestors lie in an orderly row. She started preaching in her teens, and had set her sights on becoming a missionary in the hills of Kasia, India. She went to Carmarthen College to prepare, and there she met her husband. The chance of going to Kasia disappeared, but her ardent religious zeal did not diminish.

My father, Gwyn, was born and brought up in Pentre, and he had a Welsh-speaking upbringing at a time when the chapel was a hive of activity throughout the week, offering a rich blend of culture and religion.

'Are you a Jew?' is not the question I am asked most often, but 'How did your mother come to Wales?' or 'Where did your parents meet?'

I used to give fairly elementary answers to these questions in the past. My mother came to Wales before the war, having met my father at Oxford University. I knew some further details, of course, but these were largely superficial. There was quite a romantic idea that they had met between the shelves of the Ashmolean Museum, but why did they run off to get married, flouting the traditional expectations for a minister's son?

Other more difficult questions remained. Yes, my mother had fled from Germany. How and why? I knew some elements of the story, but the more I delved the more I realised that my knowledge was sketchy.

I remember going on a family holiday to Germany when I was just four or five years old. The daily ice cream from a van was the highlight, and I would not have been conscious of the fact that the Second World War had come to an end six years previously. I also had no idea that we were visiting relatives who had recently fled from East Germany.

Children, it seems, accept their surroundings with little questioning, as they know no other circumstances. When I went with my father to Swansea town centre, we would see much of it laid waste, with the market walls in ruins, and yet I did not know then of the war and the Blitz.

Similarly, I had no inkling why Eva Monika, my mother's cousin, came to see us so often in Swansea, only a vague notion that she was on holiday. She was 25 and an attractive woman. We had fine days on the beach. Later I learnt that she was, for a while, a nurse in Newport, and that she had initially come to Wales to escape from the horrors of her German wartime experience.

On another occasion, Dolly, my mother's sister, came to stay with us at Eaton Crescent, Swansea, with some of her children. At the time, my only knowledge of German consisted of a few simple rhymes, though for children language is an easy barrier to surmount. But I do remember the talking. The talking between by mother and Eva Monika; the talking between my mother and her sister, earnest, serious, endless talking. Only later could I look back and imagine the topic of conversation.

The signs were there, of course, and I would have seen and

understood them had I been a little older. In the cellar of our house were large gas masks. They were playthings then, and we scarcely thought about their real use. I was more afraid when I was carried from my bed by a hefty fireman when our chimney caught fire. Outside was the commotion of the fire brigade crew and flames shooting from the chimney.

I used to travel each day the five miles or so from the Uplands to Llwynbrwydrau, Llansamlet, to attend Lôn-las Welsh school, with the bus driving through the remains of a town centre.

Another clue to the immediate past was my attempts at shopping. I was not apparently aware that the wider world around me was English-speaking until I was sent on errands to the Uplands to buy butter, eggs and such like. Before I left home my mother would make sure I had the book of coupons, but I didn't realise that they were a means of rationing, nor why rationing was needed. I would go the Home and Colonial to buy the goods. But how could I ask for these without a word of English? Before leaving I would be taught a sentence, without understanding the individual words, and I just hoped that the correct sounds would be produced. I blurted them out as soon as I could in the shop and offered the coupons, the shopping bag and money, and somehow I would arrive home successfully, but with a sense of clumsiness.

I had no confidence in the English language for many a year. But German? My mother, I remember, taught us some rhymes. The Brahms lullaby has remained with me since:

Guten Abend, gute Nacht,
mit Rosen bedacht,
mit Näglein besteckt,
schlüpf unter die Deck!
Morgen früh, wenn Gott will,
wirst du wieder geweckt.

… tomorrow morning, if God wishes,
you'll be awoken again.

While I enjoyed the rhymes, my mother's feelings as she sang them and taught them to me must have been very different. She did not have much of a singing voice, but she had a wealth of verses, sayings and poetry quotations, and she treasured these, finding solace in a culture that still comforted her like a warm quilt, especially after fleeing.

But we would not speak German at home. Welsh was the language there, and my mother's strong German accent was for me natural and not worthy of comment. Didn't other mothers come from Germany? Rosemarie,[1] the mother of Meirion, Geraint and Rhiannon, and then Hywel and Owain, was German. There was nothing unusual in having a German mother. When we were a little older, she would try to teach some German to my brother and me, and our pocket money would depend on half-an-hour's lesson.

Gradually, our interest in our German background grew. I made several trips to East Germany with various members of the family. My first journey was with my brother Robat, when the Iron Curtain separating the Communist-ruled states of the USSR from Western Europe was still in place. Witnessing living conditions in a Communist system based on fear and suspicion was more effective than any history lesson. We visited the family home in the town of Wittenberg, which had the family name 'Bosse' on the outside, and although some modernisation had taken place, parts of the old house were still evident. We got to know Dr Jonas, my grandfather's successor in the clinic that was set up in the home, after my grandfather had been forced to give up his post as the town's hospital's head doctor, as well as others who worked and lived there, including doctors and nuns. Among these was Schwester Gaudencia, then an elderly lady, who had experienced the war years at the clinic. I corresponded with her for some time, and by struggling with her old German script I got to know more about the difficult times. We were shown around the clinic to see the rooms in the roof where the family lived, and the round room in the tower which was my mother's favourite room.

We then went to see the family grave in the town cemetery, the first of many pilgrimages. The graveyard is some distance outside the town, made pleasant by trees and surrounded by a high wall, in the middle of which is a gateway. A little to the left we came across the grave where the names of many family members are engraved on plaques set between decorative columns against a plaster wall, and in front of these are two gravestones, my grandfather's and another in memory of my grandmother.

In the village of Mühlanger, some miles away, we were welcomed by Hedwig Hache, Heken as she was known, and her family. She was the family's maid, and she played an important part in the children's upbringing and became a close friend. It is said that my grandfather bought land for them, where they now live, with a little forest behind it leading to the river Elbe. On another visit with my family we went to Kleinzerbst, a rural village, to meet Ilse Hildebrant, one of my mother's school friends. We had started to learn about the past.

The pilgrimage then extended to include Ravensbrück concentration camp. Further visits to this hell did not make it easier: the opposite in fact. No members of the family were to be seen in Wittenberg or in the surrounding area. They had all left – died, escaped, or killed.

To return to the original question. Am I a Jew? During her last illness, my mother was asked for her religious affiliation so that this could be recorded on hospital forms at Morriston. It is not surprising that she had become anti-establishment, suspicious of systems and authority. She replied truthfully, which was deeply confusing to a system that insisted on categorisation. She had, after all, been a part of a system where such a categorisation could lead to persecution and death.

Her answer, then, went along these lines: "I'm of Jewish descent, but I was brought up in a Lutheran church. I then became a member of a Baptist chapel, but I have also been interested in Buddhism and the religions of India and the Orient.'

What was put on the form? Christian, of course.

She died less than a day after this discussion. During the last years of her life she had diligently recorded her life. She had mastered an Amstrad computer, which was quite hard work compared to today's computers. She typed daily for years, copying letters and filing these with the originals. She included an index in each file and did this with the enthusiasm she had shown when cataloguing hundreds of objects for the Egypt Centre at Swansea University. She had catalogued her own life.

She did not make this apparent to us, and neither did she make it known that she had also sent a complete copy to Günther, her brother in Sweden.

During the year following my mother's death in 1998, I was summoned by Günther to visit him in Karlshamn, a small town by the sea in southern Sweden. I had to see him while he was alive, he said, as there was nothing to be gained in attending his funeral, and so it happened. He had a mountain of family papers, and we spend two days copying hundreds of pages. He also gave me other documents, and at the time I had little idea of the contents, but in the days when airlines were not as strict about the weight of your luggage, I brought them all back to Wales.

By now I had a fair grasp of German, and I spent the evening with him listening to his story. He told me about his time in a concentration camp, about the arrests and how he had survived. He related other stories about the persecution of Jews in

Wittenberg and how the family was broken up, but also how so many survived. The next generation must know about this, he said. They had lived through the most gruesome years of the century, possibly through the cruelest years ever experienced in Europe, and many had survived. The story must survive too.

I came back to Wales loaded with documents and a sense of duty. I wondered what I could do with all the papers. I started by photocopying them all, and gave a copy to my father, to my brother Robat, to my cousin Ulrich in Bielefeld, Westphalia, and to my cousin Ute in Edingen-Neckarhausen, a hamlet by the river Neckar, not far from Heidelberg.

The four of us, members of the younger generation, then met several times. How could we set about selecting and interpreting all of this? The task seemed hopeless, but we all decided to select one side of the story, and to put them all together. This was, at least, a reason – or an excuse – for several trips to Germany.

Everyday commitments unfortunately meant that nothing came of this plan. The more I procrastinated, the more the burden of duty increased and so I started selecting parts of the story some years ago, for the Welsh branch of the family, but under pressure of work – the usual excuse – the task was far from finished.

Then, towards the end of 2009, Caryl Ebenezer from the TV company Rondo asked if they could make a documentary on a part of the story. To her dismay, we refused permission for TV cameras to follow a planned family visit to Berlin and Wittenberg during Easter 2010. Nevertheless, we are now indebted to her for insisting that Nona, my daughter, and her family and myself travelled there at New Year that year. Caryl and her associates had undertaken detailed research before the journey, had come across some people who had known the family, and they had also visited Ravensbrück to seek further information. The journey was one of both pain and pleasure, and the documentary which resulted was moving.

This placed a further duty on me to finish work on my selection of the materials to hand and try to present as complete a picture as space would allow.

This work, then, is an attempt to record the experiences of some of those who have lived through the most inhumane events in Europe, and in doing so I am keeping the promise made to my uncle. Much of the history lies in shattered fragments, and many difficult questions must remain unanswered. By trying to piece the shards together, as if reconstructing windows broken during *Kristallnacht*, perhaps I shall succeed in creating some wholeness from the fragments, just as my mother would glue together parts of an old, broken Egyptian vessel to restore a form that might yet be recognisable to inhabitants of the past.

'Go not to Wittenberg'

Hamlet, Act I, Scene 2

WAS WITTENBERG ONE OF the centres of anti-Semitism in Europe? Possibly. To the casual visitor, however, today's Wittenberg is a pleasant, quiet town of around 50,000 inhabitants on the bank of the river Elbe, a part of Sachsen-Anhalt province, around 50 miles to the south of Berlin. Tourists from all parts of the world come to visit the churches that were at the centre of the Protestant Reformation, to soak up the atmosphere of places where Martin Luther and his friends lived and worked and to acknowledge Wittenberg's place at the centre of Europe's history and religion over the past 500 years.

It is not surprising, however, that some members of our family have mixed feelings about Wittenberg. Although the family on both my grandparents' sides had settled here for a generation or two and had played a full part in the life of the town, they were persecuted as Nazism gripped the country. Because of this, none of my close family has stayed there, and some do not want to return at all, either from anger or to avoid memories of a painful past.

Until fairly recently Wittenberg was a university town. It is a one-street town in the sense that most of its important buildings are on the main street, which starts by the castle church, the Schloßkirche, where Luther nailed his anti-papist pronouncements on 31 October 1517, and it extends a mile to the corner where, with students in train just as mice and children followed the Pied Piper of Hamelin, he burned the Pope's edicts.

Robat
Gruffudd
with two of
his nieces,
Efa and
Anna, in
Wittenberg,
2010

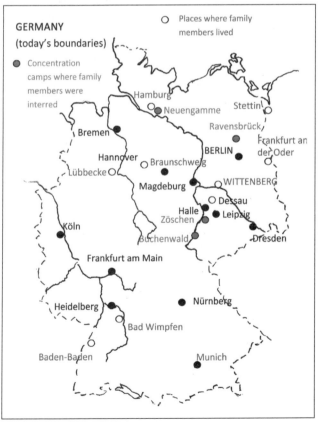

GERMANY
(today's boundaries)

○ Places where family
   members lived

● Concentration
   camps where family
   members were
   interred

Hamburg
Neuengamme
Stettin
Ravensbrück
Bremen
Frankfurt an
der Oder
Hannover
Braunschweig
BERLIN
Lübbecke
Magdeburg
WITTENBERG
Dessau
Halle
Leipzig
Köln
Zöschen
Buchenwald
Dresden
Frankfurt am Main
Heidelberg
Nürnberg
Bad Wimpfen
Baden-Baden
Munich

Other streets form half a web around the main square – in one direction streets lead to the park, which once formed a ditch around the town, and then to the main road, the railway and the river Elbe. In this web, at Heubnerstraße, number 26, was the home of Paul Bosse, my grandfather, and his family. Nearby was the hospital, Paul-Gerhardt-Stift, where he worked as a senior surgeon.

In the row of buildings facing the square and the town hall is the Goldener Adler Hotel where, it is claimed, Luther enjoyed his beer, and nearby is 82 Collegien Straße where the Bosse family ran a wine shop. A little further, still on the right, is the home of Melanchthon the theologian, now a museum, and towards the end of the street, again on the right, are the buildings of Wittenberg University where Martin Luther started lecturing in 1508. This again is a museum and includes Luther's living quarters.

To understand the attitude of Wittenberg people to the Jews one needs to delve into the town's history – not that Wittenberg people were so different to others in Germany, but the town's past can explain some of the virulent anti-Semitism seen there and in the country generally.

There is some uncertainty as to when Wittenberg was established. There is mention of 'Wittenburg' around 1180 after a period of period of conflict between the Germanic people and the Sorbs, of Slavic descent, who are still a linguistic minority in eastern parts of Germany.[2] The Germans were led by a powerful trio, including Heinrich der Löwe, Harry the Lion, from Braunschweig. After a period of flooding in the Netherlands, Flemish people settled in the villages vacated by the Slavs, and they were skilled at adapting the marshlands of the river Elbe.

It was the Flemish, it seems, who built the first defences around today's castle square. Gradually the village grew and became home to the Saxe-Wittenberg dukes and a centre of government, culture and religion for the area. In 1293 Duke Albrecht II gave

Town square shops

Martin Luther's grave in the *Schloßkirche*

Wittenberg *civitas* status, that of a town or city, and the town became self-governing. At the same time brick defences were built instead of the previous wooden ones, and the town church, the *Stadtkirche*, was extended.

The Jews had settled there as early as this period and had their own part of town, where Jüdenstraße is today. They did not have rights of citizenship, but paid protection money to the district ruler. They faced religious opposition, just as in England a century earlier, where 150 Jews gathered in York castle to escape from a threatening crowd and committed suicide rather than give up their faith. The Crusades were responsible for whipping up hatred against the Jews. By 1304, Jews were ordered to leave Wittenberg and Saxe-Wittenberg province amid worries about their financial power, and at a time when craftsmen's guilds feared competition. The guilds insisted that their members should be German-speaking and this kept the Slavs and the Jews out. Those who used Slavic languages were punished. It is not difficult for us in Wales to understand how this could happen.

Within a century, Wittenberg's defences had been strengthened, with walls and towers giving the town protection against attacks by neighbours during a period of regular conflict. By now the Jews once again inhabited their own area in the northern part of the town. The town fell to the hands of Friedrich der Streitbare of Meissen, who defeated the armed forces of the Hussites of Bohemia. Jan Hus, a theologian from Prague, had ventured to challenge the infallibility of the Pope and had attacked the wealth of the Vatican, as Luther would do a century later. Hus was burnt for heresy in 1415. After losing the battle, the Hussite forces approached Wittenberg and reached the town gate with 1,000 men. This movement was national in spirit, but it also opposed the feudal system. Once again it was defeated, but after 1433 a period of peace followed between the Hussites and Friedrich der Sanftmütige (the Gentle).

The *Stadtkirche* was extended and consecrated in 1439, but the battle against the Hussites had been expensive for the town. When this was followed by further battles against members of the same family and then against the Stellmeisen marauders, a large debt was accumulated until Friedrich III (*der Weise* – the Wise) came to live in Wittenberg in 1486 and built extensively. His masterpiece was a palace of which the castle church, the *Schloßkirche*, is a part, and later Luther and Melanchthon were buried there.

Under Friedrich's leadership, the University of Wittenberg was built and opened in 1502. Given the history of fighting the Hussites, Friedrich could hardly have imagined that this university would become central to anti-papist Christianity as a result of the work of two of its academics. Around the same time the town hall near the market square was built, and by 1553, the main buildings seen in the town today were in place.

Martin Luther:
against Pope and Jew?

Martin Luther was appointed professor of theology in 1508, and Philipp Melanchthon professor of Greek in 1518. These two became the founders of the Protestant Reformation that quickly spread across northern Europe during the 16th century. Although there was no intention of splitting the Catholic Church – but rather to criticize some of its financial practices – the result was separation. Luther did not refrain from attacking the Pope:

> One of the first things that must be done is to expel all of the Pope's missionaries from every one of Germany's territories – them and all the evil that follows them... The only thing that they do is to teach us the learning of the devil, and take money for teaching us to sin and lead us to hell. This work in itself is enough to prove that the Pope is the Antichrist.[3]

Luther's 95 proclamations were nailed to the door of the *Schloßkirche* in Wittenberg on the eve of the All Saints' festival in 1517, in opposition to the selling of indulgences. By selling these, the Pope offered forgiveness and a path to heaven to Catholics, but the indulgences were a means for the Catholic Church to raise money to build St Peter's Church in the Vatican.

There is evidence that Luther's proclamations were nailed on the doors of other churches as well. It seems that it was a custom to put pronouncements on the doors of churches, to instigate debate in a period when books were still a rarity. Eventually, Luther translated the Bible to German so that people could read it for themselves. He wrote hymns and led a protest movement that grew into the Protestant Church. His influence spread throughout the whole of northern Europe. In spite of his strongly-held views, he would hardly have thought at the time that this would have led to the establishment of a church that was independent of the Catholic Church.

Luther then led his students along the main road, past the town square and university, to a corner at the far end of the town and held a burning ceremony – the burning of the Pope's decrees. If you go there today, you can see an oak tree – the *Luthereiche* – planted on that spot to mark the event.

Every movement can benefit from a propagandist, and Luther was served by Lucas Cranach, the best available, who became a renowned artist. In 1504 he was employed as a court artist by Friedrich III, but he also became a successful businessman and established a painting school and a printing press as well as running other businesses, including a wine tavern and a pharmacy. He became the head of the town council. His pictures are seen in art galleries throughout Europe, and among his famous paintings are portraits of Martin Luther and his wife Katharina.

The Luther Oak, *die Luthereiche*

When Luther translated the New Testament to German, Cranach made 21 woodcuts for the edition printed in 1522. Books were the revolutionary technology of the sixteenth century, and Luther and Cranach were at the forefront of the new developments. During that century, half of all German books were printed in Wittenberg. Luther finished translating the Bible into German in 1534, leading to translations into other languages, including Welsh.

Behind the houses on one side of the square is the town church, the *Stadtkirche* where Luther would preach a total of 2,000 sermons, and where paintings by Lucas Cranach showing Luther at work surround the altar. Less comforting is the sculpture just below the roof of the church displaying Jews sucking the breasts of a large sow, the *Judensau*, with a rabbi raising the sow's tail. It is a symbol of the anti-Semitism of the 14th century which still persisted in the 16th century, with Luther as a fervent protagonist. He showed contempt towards the Talmud, the Jewish legal scripts, and said in reference to the sculpture of the large sow, that Jews should 'eat and drink the letters that drop' from under the sow's tail. The image of the sow is seen on more than 20 of Germany's churches, and the word 'Judensau' was used by the Nazis when referring to Jews.

In 1543 Luther authored a 60,000-word book, *On the Jews and their Lies,* published by Hans Lufft in Wittenberg.[4] In it he described the Jews as 'base, prostitute people, and not the people of God'. He said that they were 'full of the devil's excreta… they wallow in it like pigs'.

He formed a seven-point plan against the Jews, and urged the burning of their synagogues and schools, and the confiscation of their books and writings. He urged the destruction of their prayer books and said that rabbis should be prohibited from preaching. In addition, their houses should be burnt and their possessions and money taken, without mercy, and they should be prohibited

The *Judensau* sculpture

Luther's book, *On the Jews and their Lies,* 1543
A Nazi booklet quoting Luther

Luther's 95 theses on the door of the *Schloßkirche*, with a picture of him and Melanchthon by the cross

The town church, *die Stadtkirche*

from lending money. Jews and Jewesses should earn their living through sweat, using the axe and hoe, spade and spinning wheel. Luther justified his arguments by claiming that Jews crucified Christ and had refused to accept him as the Messiah. This was a common position at the time, and it is certain that the anti-Semitism of the Catholic Church had influenced him.

Luther had hoped to convert Jews to Christianity and argued that they were of the same blood as Christ. He acknowledged that priests and monks had treated Jews as if they were dogs rather than people, but he became bitter after failing to attract them to the Christian faith and pronounced that he would baptize Jews by lowering them into the river Elbe, with heavy stones around their necks.

This is not the Luther who is so respected in Wales for translating the Bible into German, for hymn-writing and for leading the Protestant Reformation. This anti-Jewish Luther is a fount of vile ideas.

Four centuries after Luther's propaganda, the Nazis took advantage of his stance. They could justify their anti-Semitism by quoting the founder of Protestantism. They published a booklet using Luther's exhortations, and extended his arguments into the 20th century: 'Away with them' is the alarming incitement.

When one considers Luther's efforts to throw the Jews out of Sachsen and many German towns, it is not surprising that the Nazis were glad to be able to use him as an example and as a basis for their own deviant beliefs.

A possible contemporary to Luther in Wittenberg was the famous Faust. Dr Johann Georg Faust (c. 1480–1540) was a scientist of some kind, and his exploits as a magician and alchemist became the subject of Marlowe's play, *The Tragicall History of the Life and Death of Doctor Faustus* (1604) and later, Goethe's well-known play, *Faust* (1808). There is mention of Dr Faust in Heidelberg and he is connected with other places including Bamberg and

Nürnberg. History and fable are easily entwined. In one version of the story, Johann Faust is a son of a peasant who went on to study theology, medicine and witchcraft in Wittenberg. His urge is to collect all knowledge, and he enters into a contract with the devil, Mephistopheles, in a forest near Wittenberg. Goethe uses this background early in his play.

Goethe's *Faust* was translated into Welsh by Lewis Edwards in *Y Traethodydd* at the end of the 19th century, with another translation by T. Gwynn Jones at the start of the 20th century and a later translation again by R. Gerallt Jones.[5]

Since Martin Luther's time, Wittenberg has become more of a backwater, but Luther still exerts his influence on the town, as he has done for some 500 years. His work literally towers above the town, as the words of his famous hymn, 'Ein feste Burg ist unser Gott' ('A mighty fortress is our God', translated into Welsh by Lewis Edwards as 'Ein nerth a'n cadarn dŵr yw Duw') are written in broad letters across the tower of the castle's church.

Remarkably, at exactly the same period as Wales was incorporated into England through the 1536 Act of Union, Wittenberg was part of the reforms and changes that within 50 years would contribute massively to diminishing the effect of that anti-Welsh law.

Wales has somehow continued to survive from one crisis to another, and probably will continue to do so, but it is not an exaggeration to claim that the Welsh language would not have lived on without the events at Wittenberg. William Morgan would probably not have translated the Bible into Welsh by 1588 if Martin Luther had not translated the Bible into German half a century earlier. When Protestantism spread across Europe, the London parliament in 1563 passed a law to translate the Bible into Welsh and acknowledged that Welsh-medium resources were needed for the new religion to be accepted in Wales. In the wake of the partial collapse of the power of the Catholic

Church, the national languages of Europe could find new strength through becoming the language of religion, and consequently the language of learning.

The tragedy of the Welsh language is that it accepted mandatory English-medium education during the period of mass immigration in the 19th century. This was at a time when a large proportion of the population were monolingual Welsh speakers and literate in their language, thanks to the circulating schools of Griffith Jones and the Sunday schools of Thomas Charles. The Welsh Bible was the basis of religion in Wales, and also in its wake the voluntary education system that made the Welsh literate.

From a personal standpoint, of course, the influence of Wittenberg on the Welsh language continued when my mother came to Wales, raised a Welsh-speaking family, contributed to the country's literature and took part in many language campaigns and in several Welsh national movements.

Luther's memorial on the market quare, with the town church in the background

Wars and Communism

GERMANY EXPERIENCED MANY WARS during the following centuries. The Thirty Years' War (1618–48) was especially damaging; to some extent it was a battle between Protestants and Catholics, and it was a particularly unfortunate result of the religious reformation. Spain, France, Sweden and Denmark took part in the fighting. It is estimated that Germany lost between 15 and 30 per cent of its population during the conflict, and many areas of the country were impoverished, including Wittenberg. The next century saw the Seven Years' War (1756–63), and more destruction. The forces of Austria and Saxony attacked the town and burnt the castle and the *Schloßkirche*.

Some rebuilding took place – but then Napoleon passed through Wittenberg on 22 October 1806, during his march to Russia. A row of trees which he planted still exists. The electorate of Saxony decided to support Napoleon and the town found itself having to contribute a great deal of food and drink to the army. With French soldiers in the town, a part of the castle was converted into a military hospital and when Napoleon failed in his attempt to reach Moscow in 1812, Prussian and Russian forces attacked and burned the castle and the church once again in 1814. The castle had by then become a military barracks for German forces. As a result of the war, the town's population fell from 7,100 to 4,800.

Following this period of decline, the town gradually grew and once again became a centre of trade and industry. Unlike the tendency in previous centuries, Wittenberg managed to avoid much damage in the 1914–18 war, but this was followed by a

The town square where Napoleon once drilled his soldiers. The fine town hall is still here, and in front of it are statues of Martin Luther and Melanchthon

period of severe economic and social difficulties which the whole of Germany had to face.

The Second World War

To many inhabitants, the reign of the Nazis marked a period of oppression from their own government. But in the unstable period following the First World War, conditions were ripe for the rise of the Nazi party. Germans were angry with the onerous terms of the Treaty of Versailles which ended the conflict. Under these Germany was forced to disarm, make substantial territorial concessions and pay billions of Marks in reparations. Between 1921 and 1924, three years of hyperinflation under the Weimar Republic wiped out people's savings as money became virtually valueless. The conditions were auspicious for a revolution.

That revolution came as the Nazis became the largest political party. There is little to be gained in arguing that the Nazi party never gained a majority of votes. It is rare that any party has a majority of votes in a general election in the UK, but this does not prevent it from governing. So it was in Germany. When Hitler came to power, he set about reviving the economy, building highways and giving work to a generation who had been without hope. In time, the Ruhr, which was so important to the economy and self-respect of the Germans, was retaken from its Franco-Belgian occupiers. His popularity was no surprise. The catastrophe was his abuse of power, the urge to expand German territory through military means, his extreme racism and the insane aspiration to see himself as the leader of the 'Thousand-Year Reich'. All of which culminated in the killing of millions of Jews and another world war.

Many SS and SA soldiers were stationed in Wittenberg in 1922 after Hitler had won power, starting the darkest period in the town's history. The SS were the *Schutzstaffel* (the protection brigade) who belonged to the Nazi Party, and the SA were the *Sturmabteilung* (the storm troopers), the paramilitary section of the Nazi organisation. Wittenberg had willing supporters of the Nazis and they were later given freedom to persecute the town's Jewish population, both before and during the Second World War.

The Communist Regime

At the end of the war, with the Russians reaching Wittenberg across the river Elbe, Wittenberg found itself part of communist East Germany. Even after the war, this internal oppression was followed by external oppression as the Russian army was stationed in the town. The Russians were seen as aggressors, and they dealt their share of revenge. Women were raped by soldiers. Men who tried to defend women were shot. A tank was placed opposite the *Schloßkirche* as a symbol of 'freeing' the town by the Russians. Gradually the communist system established order, although that order was based on surveillance and lack of freedom of expression and movement, and often on fear.

In 1946, the 400th anniversary of Luther's death was marked

A Russian tank in front of the castle church

by reopening his home in the university to the public. In 1967, alongside celebrating Karl Marx and Lenin, Luther's contribution to improving the lives of peasants was recognised, and the 450th anniversary of nailing the proclamations on the church door was celebrated, and then the 500th anniversary of Luther's birth was celebrated in 1983.

The positive developments during years of communist rule included building an Olympic-size swimming pool in nearby Piesteritz, along with building schools, houses and factories which gave everyone the certainty of work. By 1979 the Soviet tank unit left Wittenberg and a shop opened where people could buy Western goods with Western money, which they probably obtained on the black market.

The town centre of Wittenberg, however, had an impoverished look by the 1970s. Paint and building materials were scarce and buildings deteriorated. By the time of the celebrations of 1983, a substantial part of the main street was renovated to become a shop window for tourists, and from then on things gradually got better. Oranges were still in short supply in the fruit shop in the town centre – they were hard and greenish and came from Cuba. Visitors from Western Europe would have a feast for breakfast in the Adler Hotel, with a banana served on a silver plate, while East German workers would have a bun and a boiled egg.

Wittenberg, following the establishment of a peace movement there in the 1980s, was heavily involved in the democratic revolution that swept away the communist state and led eventually to the reunification of Germany. In 1983 a sword was symbolically beaten into a ploughshare before 2,000 observers from the Congress of Protestant Churches. Although the meeting had been prohibited, the Stasi – the country's secret police – looked on powerlessly. During the following years the Church had a central role in the effort to establish democracy in Germany, and numerous meeting were held in both of the town's churches

A shop selling oranges from Cuba, Wittenberg, 1981

Wittenberg's main street, with the castle church at its far end, in 1981

during 1989. In September 1989 meetings were held in the market square and some 10,000 inhabitants gathered to nail seven proclamations on the town hall door in a symbolic act.

This contributed to the pressure which made it impossible for East Germany to continue within the communist system. The Berlin Wall, which had divided the city since 13 August 1961, was opened due to a misunderstanding on 9 November 1989. Within a year it had been demolished after Germany was reunified in October 1990. A banana stall came to Wittenberg's town hall square for the first time, and the town then saw substantial changes. The negative side included unemployment, as factories which could not compete in the open market were forced to close. On the positive side, substantial rebuilding and renovation took place, and the town today has first-class hotels which attract visitors to one of Europe's most important centres of learning and religion.

Paul and Kaethe Bosse and their family in Wittenberg

IT IS IMPOSSIBLE TO foresee how one would react in a period of crisis. In Wales we have the comfort of being able to take part in protests or oppose politicians freely, in the knowledge that we would not face much suffering because of it. Such opposition could mean one not being appointed to a certain post, perhaps, or failing to climb the ranks of establishments favoured by the party in power. It is possible to imagine, on the other hand, that those who support certain politicians, more out of self-interest than principle, can obtain posts beyond their merit, with no obstacles to promotion. Perhaps that is why so many leaders of Welsh public life and Welsh institutions are so lacking in talent.

It is worth considering how we would react if our rights to express our opinions or take part in politics were severely restricted. It is much more difficult to imagine how we would react if these restrictions were extended to our daily life because of our family tree.

Paul Bosse and his wife Kaethe, née Ledien, would hardly have thought about such matters before 1933, just as we do not imagine that our political system will be turned upside down and run by a racist dictator. Would they try to oppose the system, or toe the line? Perhaps there would be no freedom of choice. Opposition would mean exclusion from society or even imprisonment. Survival, surely, was the common aim of the majority. Many survived by becoming supporters of Hitler. That was not a path chosen by Paul and Kaethe Bosse. To what extent was compliance a possibility? The answer would come during the following years.

Paul Bosse and Kaethe Ledien were raised during the last years of the 19th century. Wittenberg was a university town, and the students' antics attracted attention now and again. Among the family's papers is a 24-page description of the town by Hans Ledien, Kaethe's brother, written on the request of his nephew Günther, my mother's brother.

At the time Wittenberg had around 20,000 inhabitants, and in their midst was the 20th regiment of the *Infanterie-Regiment Graf Tauentzien* and the 4th cavalry of the *Feldeartillerie-Regiments* (Prinz-Regent Luitpold von Bayern).

The town was comparatively military in nature therefore, and soldiers would be seen regularly around the town, partly because of the numerous restaurants and public houses and also because of the brewery. Farmers from the surrounding countryside would also take advantage of the eating and drinking opportunities when they came to the market, especially during periods of festivals. Stalls at that time would be erected on the castle square and also on the main street, where shoes for farmers would be sold, with clothes stalls on the market square, and the children would buy multi-coloured sugar sticks for five Pfennigs. *Speckkuchen* – a cake containing bacon, and sometimes eggs and onions – was a speciality of local bakeries.

Land workers from Poland and Ruthenia were among the shoppers, and they wore colourful traditional garments. When they bought three Marks of goods with Max Salzmann (whose shop was at Markt 1), they would get a free bread roll and a glass of beer. The town at that time had three good hotels, including the Goldener Adler, which is still there.

The town was a pleasant one, according to Hans, with several factories in the vicinity, whose products included tiles, explosives, soap, marble and beer. The Bosse distillery was among the smaller producers. Hans states, 'Julius Bosse [the father of Paul Bosse] was well-off financially because of this. I was very fond of the two large black horses which the coachman Kulisch would drive, pulling the company's produce carriages on workdays.' On Sundays the carriages would have black and yellow cushions.

As in other parts of Germany, a shooting festival would be held annually, and the greatest honour was to be appointed *Schützenkönig*, the king of the shoot. Julius Bosse, who was by now a town councillor, was given this honour, although he did not take part in the shooting. He had to pay the costs of the honour, a 'royal' feast. The festival would last a week, a carnival for Wittenberg people.

Only 25 years had passed since the town walls had been demolished, and the town had not expanded much since then. The local court, hardly a comfortable place, was in the town hall until a new court was built in 1909. There was also a town bank and a town cellar (used as a restaurant), and there were shops around the square.

There were between six and eight policemen, 'and *Paukenschmidt* [Schimdt the drummer] was particularly popular. Schmidt was his name, and he used to carry the regiment's large drum'. During the evening nightwatchmen would take the place of the policemen, and these had their own uniforms, with a cap instead of the policeman's helmet. Part of their work was to light the gas lamps on the street, using long sticks. Confrontations could arise as overenthusiastic students set about pestering them on 'Wittenberg Academic Evening'. Fritzsche, one of the watchmen, was often drunk, and Hans remembers an evening celebrating his *Abitur* (the school higher certificate) with 400 friends enjoying beer and rolls, to the accompaniment of the regiment band.

On his way home Hans saw a man lying on the ground. It was Fritzsche, the nightwatchman.

On one occasion school students put a ladder up against Luther's monument on the square, climbed it and placed a tankard of beer on the monument's plinth. When Paul Bosse was a student, the revellers of the Wittenberg Academic Evenings dragged the shooting festival's stall and placed it across Elbe Street, closing it. But as there were no cars in Wittenberg at that time, no harm was done.

Heubnerstraße, the street where the family lived, did not exist in 1900. The hospital, the Paul-Gerhardt-Stift, was not built at its present site until 1909. The town's grammar school – the *Gymnasium* – had been built on its new site in 1888. (The school has now moved to a building designed by the artist Hundertwasser.) Earlier it was held in buildings on the church square.

If you came across Paul Bosse and Kaethe Ledien in Wittenberg at the turn of the 20th century, you would see two handsome, affluent young people, both having been raised in well-off homes. Paul could trace his German ancestry to the 17th century, while Kaethe belonged to a fairly wealthy family of Jewish extraction.

Julius Heinrich Wilhelm Bosse, Paul's father, was born in Braunschweig in 1838. He died comparatively young at the age of 59, when Paul was just 17. He ran a business supplying wine and beer in Wittenberg, and inhabitants still recall his recipe for beer, which they called 'Bossebier'; this recipe went to the grave with him. His business was at 82 Collegienstraße, within 100 yards of the town square, and not far from the Adler Hotel. Julius's father, Elias Friedrich Wilhelm Bosse, was a skilled furniture maker, and some of his furniture is still in the possession of members of the family. Paul's mother was Amalie Pauline Josephine Waymeyer. She was born in 1851, and it is predominantly members of her side of the family who are to be found in the family grave in Wittenberg.

Max Levin, Kaethe's father, was a solicitor, or to give him his full title, a Councillor and Royal Notary of the King of Prussia. He was born in 1856 in Frankfurt an der Oder, which today lies on the border with Poland but was at that time in Brandenburg province, in the centre of the kingdom of Prussia. Max was 30 years of age when Kaethe Levin was born. He belonged to a family of Jews who had already turned to the Christian faith, as was the trend among so many German Jews. Kaethe's mother, Luise Hedwig Alexander, was born in Berlin in 1863, and was descended from a Jewish family.

On the *Ahnenpass,* the ancestry documents which Günther Bosse, their grandson and Kate's brother, had to complete during the Nazi period, Max Levin is noted as 'mosaisch', the term used on certificates for 'Jewish', but it also notes 'später Dissident' ('later a dissident'). The same is noted for his wife, Luise Alexander.

The confirmation of Kaethe Levin, their daughter, into the Lutheran Church took place on 21 March 1901, when she was 15 years old, in the town church, the *Stadtkirche,* in Wittenberg. The whole family had previously been baptized in 1896. Günther's *Ahnenpass* notes that Kaethe was a member of the Lutheran Church, denoted by 'ev', for 'evangelisch', but the town official has also written 'früher mosaisch' – 'earlier Jewish', next to this. This is unlikely to be true, and is probably an attempt to note her ancestry.

Paul was clearly anxious to find out whether his wife, Kaethe, was of 'pure' Jewish descent. He managed to find that a French admiral, who was a pure 'Aryan', was among the forefathers of his wife, but this made no difference to the treatment she received later.

How aware was the family of anti-Semitic sentiments, and did this influence them to turn to the Christian church? Anti-Semitism was rampant in many parts of Europe, especially in the eastern lands in Europe. Many Jews in Germany had freed themselves from their tradition, had accepted Christianity and had taken the opportunity to give themselves a more Germanic name. That was the case of Kaethe's parents. The 'Levin' or 'Levien' found on certificates was changed to 'Ledien', to distance themselves from the Jewish 'Levi', and by the turn of the 20th century the family was Christian.

Paul and Kaethe were married on 3 April 1906 in Wittenberg. By now Paul was working as a doctor and in 1907 employed as a surgeon in the Paul-Gerhardt-Stift hospital, which was sponsored by the church.

Their hopes for the future must have been great and numerous. They had children swiftly. Dolly, their shortened name for Dorothea, was the eldest. She was born in 1907 and, in time, became a doctor.

Kate, born in 1910, was the second daughter. Her future interest was in the ancient world, and she obtained a doctorate from Munich University on Egyptian sculpture. Günther was born in 1913, and he too became a doctor. Fritz, born in 1915, was the youngest son. He eventually became a farmer and an inventor of farm machinery.

After their marriage, Kaethe's main work was looking after the home, as was the custom of the time, especially for wives with a comfortable home background. Her interests were expansive: she had spent a period in England mastering her command of English, which would be useful in times to come when she took advantage of her English contacts. She raised their children with the help of a faithful family maid, Hedwig Hache, or Heken as she was also called. Painting was among her interests, and some of her pictures have survived.

This peaceful family life would not last long. When the First World War broke out, Paul was called to serve as a medical officer with the German army. The evidence is that he did his utmost for his country. He won a rescue medal for saving lives

Paul Bosse around 1910

Kaethe Bosse with Dolly, her daughter, around 1910

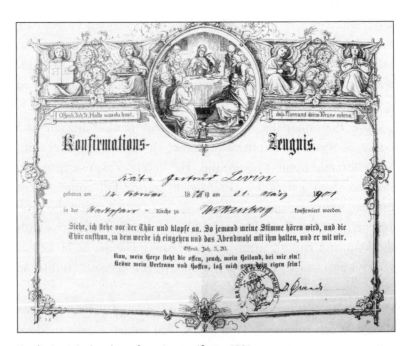

Kaethe Levin's church confirmation certificate, 1901

and a DSC of the German Red Cross for his surgical work. However, he was seriously injured and suffered some damage to his heart and was released from front-line service, being 50 per cent disabled. He survived, but others in the family were not as fortunate. Friedrich, Kaethe's brother, was killed in the fighting on 13 November 1916. Another brother, Hans, was a front-line officer from 1914 to 1918, and later became a lawyer in Wittenberg. Eva, Kaethe's sister, was married to a senior officer in the military who later became an army general in Berlin. Being married to persons of Jewish extraction, or being Jewish, was no hindrance to serving Germany in that war.

After Paul was released from military service, and with the family now living in a larger home at 26 Heubnerstraße to which they moved from a flat near the main square in 1915, Paul Bosse could take up his duties once more at the Wittenberg hospital. From 1919 to 1935 he was the hospital's senior doctor. His son Günther remembered seeing him in a doctor's uniform and almost never in ordinary clothes.[6] He also had private patients, and two rooms in the cellar of the extensive house were given over for this work.

It was clear to his small son that Paul went about his work earnestly. The family had to take meals at particularly punctual times, with all the family present, and Kaethe would make every effort to give her husband her best attention. Paul's expectations could be demanding, as he was sensitive to various foods. He would eat quickly and disappear to his work as soon as the meal was over.

But for years, according to Günther, lunchtime would be interrupted by phone calls from the health officer – calls which would last a long time as it was easier to get hold of Paul Bosse at home than in the hospital.

Günther portrays him as being strict and authoritarian; perhaps this was the custom of the age: the head of family held sway. Paul

Dolly and Kate and their mother, Kaethe Bosse
Kaethe with her two daughters, Dolly and Kate,
February 1913

Paul Bosse's war disability card in 1942, noting that he had been injured in the
First World War

would quickly fly into a rage if the family was late for a meal, and
his wife Kaethe would be the one to suffer. On the other hand,
according to Günther, she was sensitive and easily wounded,
although her niece Erika, the daughter of her brother Hans,

describes her differently: 'I was fond of visiting Oma ['granny', used by the family for Kaethe], who was so welcoming and lively, and who was optimistic in outlook, unlike my mother who could not hide her fear and worries.'

At home Paul was the centre of attention, but he could also be kind and generously supportive. But if the children misbehaved, a clout about the ears was the order before any explanation could be given. He would insist on high standards of honour. Once a friend of the boys was suspected of stealing some objects from the house. Paul left paper money on the table before he arrived. The money disappeared, and the boy was not allowed into the house again. According to Günther, he could treat people harshly, even with contempt, but at other times he would be sympathetic and understanding.

Günther remembers another incident:

> A visitor had come, and he was welcomed to the lounge. Kate – although she was just ten years old – was given the task of cutting an apple on a delicate plate. She succeeded so well that the plate split in two… My father reacted at once with a clout.

On the other hand, Günther remembers going with him to the hospital many times:

> I could go with him often to visit the patients, as part of his duties; so we would go not only to hospital, but also to various places in the community, where less fortunate young people would be housed; in homes for orphans and so on.

Günther's fondest memories of his boyhood are of Sundays during Advent, when Paul would spend the whole day with the children. They would play games, sing carols, and much more.

After the First World War, the family bought a car, and they would go on carefully planned trips, taking baskets of food.

The children would be given pocket money, but they would have to work for this in the garden and around the house. When

Paul Bosse with Günther, his son, around 1920

Günther was old enough, one of his duties was shovelling several tons of coal for the heating system from the street through a window in the cellar.

The family had a large garden in a nearby street – Kurfürstenstraße – and although most of the land had been let to others, there was enough left for the family to grow potatoes, berries of all kinds, plums and so on. Paul was very proud of the asparagus beds that he had laid, and this pride would be shown by the children when their turn came to harvest these. He gave the children the best opportunities. The grammar school – *Melanchthongymnasium* – was for boys only. But Paul insisted that his daughters went there, contrary to the expectations of the period. Dolly was the only girl there when she started attending the school. Kate later joined her, and it was there that she received her grounding in the Classics.

It was not possible, however, to escape the effects of the First World War. At the end of the war, Wittenberg, like many other places in Germany, suffered as France occupied the country's western regions and as the supply of goods decreased. This was followed by hyperinflation. Some of this is recorded in Kate's diaries, when she was just 13:

15 January 1923

The French keep doing nasty things to us. Now they have an army in Essen, and apart from this they have occupied other cities. This was against the peace agreement. This will be very harmful for industry. Today there was a mourning service in every school because of this. Vati [Dad] believes that the French are occupying... perhaps because there will be another war with Russia, and there could be considerable time before that... The French claim (as far as I understand) that they are doing this because Germany has not sent them enough coal and wood.

Tante Eva has been for some time with Jochen in Gleiwitz. They and Onkel Will are afraid that the Poles will occupy Gleiwitz.

Tante Eva, Kaethe's sister, was married to Willibald Borowietz who was a military officer. He came from Breslau, which is now in Poland, now known as Wroclaw. They had one son, Jochen (Joachim), at that time. Entries in Kate's diaries portray how things worsened during the following months.

8 March 1923

Things are going from bad to worse with the French. They have occupied the whole Ruhr country and are refusing coal trains to go to parts of Germany which have not been occupied. They are going around like wild animals. Every day there is mention of more murders and people being thrown out. This persecution, often of mayors and of coal mine owners, happens as these are taken away in cars and are dropped off by the border, without being able to take anything with them. The anger of Ruhr area workers is forever increasing, and it is a wonder that no riot has occurred. For how long can this continue? Many meetings have been arranged already to support them. But it is not possible for them to come to German land. Because England and America, the only countries who could do something against this, are watching idly on to see what will happen. Sweden is helping through financial aid. The French are being hated more and more.

The German opposition to its treatment at the hands of the French is noted by Kate some two months later.

A picnic in the country   Paul Bosse in the family garden

29 April 1923

Everywhere where this can harm the French, bridges are exploded in spite of the supervision…

Then, some months later, the Wittenberg area is affected as children from the Ruhr are sent to the town for refuge.

12 June 1923

Tuesday

One Saturday, Sunday and Monday, because we had school holidays, I was with the Hildebrants. On the Saturday children from the Ruhr district arrived. There were ten of them in all in Kleinzerbst. The Hildebrants accepted two sisters, Paula and August. When they came they wept the first evening. And if one hated the French before this, one could certainly do so now. When you think that it is all the fault of the French that children are taken away from their region and parents for an indeterminate and long time, perhaps.

Ilse Hildebrant was one of Kate's school friends, and she lived in the small village of Kleinzerbst. Kate then describes a conversation she had one afternoon with the children from the Ruhr:

15 June 1923

On Sunday Paula, Ilse and I went to the meadow, and August – a boy from Essen – was in the village at the time. He had settled down well. We had blankets. Ilse, Lena and Paula and I were lying together. We were a little distance from each other and we would talk in pairs. Paula and I were talking about the French. She told me what a mess the French were creating in Essen. Often they would break into shops and ruin them. At night they are usually drunk and fighting with each other in the street and so on. They insist that everyone around them in the street greets them. But in spite of that little children sing in the street:

> Franzose weine nicht
> Ruhrkohle kriegst Du nicht
> Setz Dir den Stahlhelm auf
> Und geht nach Haus

> [Frenchman, do not weep
> You won't have Ruhr coal
> Wear your steel helmet
> And go home]

If adults did this, they would be thrown into prison. But many girls forget, and go out and flirt with the Frenchmen. If this is seen, people cut their hair off. But this can lead to shooting, because the

Ilse Hildebrant, who lived in Kleinzerbst in 1982

59

French want to defend the girls. At the beginning they had been quite friendly, offering chocolate to the children. So it was with Paula's sister. But she had not taken it, because she knew what was behind this.

The French threw more and more people out of the Ruhr district and they have already sentenced three to death. The first is ready to die a hero.

By 1923 rampant inflation had wreaked havoc with Germany's economic system, with money losing its value by the hour. Kate notes in her diary how payment for hospital care rose from 3.50 Marks in 1920 to 5,000,000 Marks by 1 September 1923 and then to 2,870,000,000,000 Marks by the end of the year.

In 1923 an attempt was made to stabilise the value of gold, but this was not without its consequences. Kate wrote in her diary on 28 October 1923:

> There is commotion of all kinds everywhere. Here people stole from Petrik's shop, because margarine had gone too expensive to buy. In Klein Wittenberg people attacked the bakery and forced the baker to sell bread for 1 milliard instead of 6,500,000,000. Then the *Sicherheitspolizei* [security police] came and tried to disperse the crowd. They had to shoot and three people were injured and taken to custody. In Heubnerstraße [where they lived] we don't see any of the unrest which is taking place in the town.

In November 1923 the money system was reformed, and new money, the Rentenmark, was introduced, with each new Mark worth one trillion of the old paper Marks. Inflation came to an end as the Rentenmark held its ground, but the disorder had already spurred Hitler to start agitating:

> 8 December 1923
>
> Prices have become cheaper after introducing the Rentenmark. The riot had no further consequences. Then on 8 November under Ludendorff and one other there was a Putsch. But this was defeated by the *Sicherheitspolizei*.

Hitler was the 'one other' referred to. In a beer hall in Munich in 1923 he and Ludendorff attempted to unseat the government, but failed. Ludendorff opposed communism and objected fervently to the terms of the Versailles agreement, and in 1925 he stood for election against Paul von Hindenburg, but lost miserably. By 1928 he had turned his back on Hitler and the Nazi Party, but still believed that Christians, Jews and Freemasons were at the root of the world's problems.

Paul and Kaethe's four children were brought up against this background. They received a Christian upbringing in the town church, and the confirmation ceremony had more pomp than is usual in Wales.[7] By 1926 Kate was keeping a detailed diary, and this is how she described the first communion on 31 March that year:

> The communion is tomorrow… I have already had some presents beforehand, so for example three pocket handkerchiefs with lovely crotchet work by Onkel Will's mother and a pocket handkerchief from the Sister Amanda. We had supper with Oma [her grandmother] and Onkel Will and Tante Eva, and also Lieselotte. Tante and Onkel Mulzer had come to fetch Mutti [her mother] by car around 9 o'clock from the train to Oma. Then Dolly and I travelled at once to the house.
>
> In the morning I went at a quarter to nine with Vati, Mutti and the boys to church. The blessing was at 9… Even Onkel Will and Oma were at the church…
>
> At 5 the guests came, 2 Springer, 2 Dr Wachs, 2 Dr Möller, 2 Borowietz, Oma, Onkel Hanne, Tante Wanda and also naturally the Mulzers. We ate a supper we had from the Adler for hours on end. I was sitting between Vati and Mutti… There was a fine atmosphere among the whole company. To finish we even danced… At half past twelve the whole company went home. Onkel Will was very dear to me that evening. He gave me some good lessons, which I thus took to my heart, because I had experienced their truth so often. But the basic song was this: I should only be a girl, a girl who would not promote herself at all at the expense of boys.

Paul Bosse with one of his grandchildren

Kate, sitting on the font left, with her *Abitur* (advanced level) class, 1930

This awareness of a girl's inferior place in society was the basis for many of Kate's stories and novels in future years, where she discusses the role and aspiration of women.

In the course of time Paul ensured that Kate had all that was necessary for her study trips to Rome,[8] Greece and later Egypt. Günther remembers meeting her on a return journey, spending a pleasant week in Ravello. Their parents had paid for everything, including the train and hotel.

Later, when Günther embarked on his medical studies, he also was given every support, and when difficulties disrupted his career, he found work in his father's clinic.

Modernity and affluence took pride of place in Paul Bosse's daily life. His fondness for films, the new entertainment medium of the age, was shown by his purchase of a personal seat in the local cinema.

In 1931 Paul and Kaethe celebrated their silver wedding anniversary. They arranged a celebration dinner and Kaethe prepared the menu, which contained a 1925 Auslese wine, 'Wehlener Auslese', and also a 1928 wine from Rüdesheim. Both wines came from private vineyards. The first course was asparagus and tongue meat, followed by ducklings with young vegetables for the main course. Fruit, cheese and coffee followed.

Günther remembers one event which unsettled him, on the day of his wedding to Edith (24 December 1937), a Swedish girl who worked in the family home. Paul cried uncontrollably during the wedding. Günther was embarrassed by this, and could only explain it as a sense of relief that he had not married a German Aryan. The tension between those of Aryan and Jewish descent was already clear.

The 1936 Olympic Games

As will be seen, life for Paul Bosse and his family was already full of difficulties. But Paul had one opportunity to show his loyalty to his country. The Olympic Games, the 11th Olympiad, came to Germany in 1936. The decision to hold the games had already been made in 1931, during the period of the Weimar Republic, before the Nazis came to power. Taking advantage of this, Hitler was eager for these games to prove the superiority of the Aryan race over all others. Wishing to fulfil his duties as a doctor to his country, Paul Bosse became one of the medical team which served the German athletes, primarily the sprinters.

Paul described his experience during the games when he had to account for his political connection with the Third Reich:

> As an Olympic doctor, I supervised the sprint runners. In connection with this I went with many others who took part in the games, from Germany and from other countries, to a cabaret show held in the *Reichkanzlei [the Reich Chancellory]* where Hitler was also present. That was the only connection I had with the representatives of the Third Reich. Apart from that, I and all my family were persecuted, pestered, and our freedom was taken, and we lost our rights and everyone avoided us.

There had been apprehension that the world's nations would stay away from the games because of the racist policies of the Nazis. The International Olympic Committee put pressure on Germany to allow those of Jewish descent to take part. During the games, the anti-Jewish propaganda of the Nazis, including posters and graffiti, was removed.

The games were held in a newly built stadium in Berlin, holding 100,000 spectators. Nearby was a large field where Hitler would stage grandiose ceremonies to display his power.

Hitler did not succeed in his hope of Aryan superiority.

Paul Bosse's identity card for the
Berlin Olympic Games, 1936

A part of the Olympic area today

Although many Germans shone, Jesse Owens, the black athlete from the USA, was the star of the games winning gold medals in four disciplines.

Among Kate's letters of this year was one from an academic acquaintance, Arthur James, who then changed his name to Walter James, from Lewes, Sussex. It is clear that they had met in Berlin when Kate was working in the Egyptological Museum there, and that she had given him German lesson. On 6 August 1936, James says:

> I am very sorry that we failed to meet one another on the Kurfürsterdamm that evening – but the next day was quite impossible, being taken up with packing and tender farewells to No. 3 [he had three lovers, one in Denmark, one in Munich and the third in Berlin]. No doubt I shall be able to see you in England – and if you want an introduction to the British chaplain in September, you have only to write to me.
>
> I see with chagrin that the British participants in the Olympic Games are doing extraordinarily badly. Perhaps we need a little new blood in our race – for the mixed-blooded Americans are doing well as usual. It makes me laugh to see the black men beating the white men on the *Reischsportfeld* of all places. I think it is a jolly good lesson for the Americans too, for they hate their blacks enough and lynch them whenever they misbehave.
>
> I hope your plans for the English journey turn out favourably – I think you may be rather bored with England – I can't stand a country where the public houses shut at 10 p.m. and have a good mind to spend all my spare time in Germany.

Kate was soon to face the possibility of seeking refuge in England, and the Nazi system was threatening. With the Second World War came worry, sorrow and grief.

PART 2

THE PERSECUTION

The family ensnared

ANTI-SEMITISM HAD SPREAD WIDELY in Wittenberg since the early days of the Nazis. In 1921 a sign was put on the door of 52 Collegienstraße, the main street, refusing entry to Jews. A group of local Nazis was set up in the town in 1925, the year the National Party of Wales was established. A lecture was given in 1929 by Ludwig Münchmeyer, a Nazi theologian, in which he asked what Luther's attitude would have been had he lived then. Some days later, Nazis marched through the town with anti-Jewish placards, and they followed this up with leaflets condemning the Jews.

Another notable event occurred on 30 January 1933 when Nazis marched past the businesses and homes of around 70 of the town's Jews, and the SS ordered the closure of all Jewish shops. A report in the local paper noted that Jewish businesses were closed on 11 March 1933:[1]

Many Jewish businesses closed in Wittenberg
As in most similar German towns, SA and SS officers this morning closed the Jewish business in the town. They started in the market square with the Breminger and Kinski shops, then they set about closing the shops of Israel, Hirschfeld, Rosen and Borinski with immediate effect. Later they closed the shops of the Baumann, Webwarenhaus and other companies.

When the 450th anniversary of Luther's birth was celebrated in the same year, the Nazis compared his activities with the regeneration of Germany under Hitler. A press conference was held on 26 September 1933 in Luther's home, in which Bishop

Joachim Hossenfelder, who was a member of the Nazi Party and the leader of a Christian anti-Jewish group, asserted that Hitler had been sent by God. The following day the National Synod of the German Protestant Church was held in Wittenberg, and the town mayor, Werner Faber, and Ludwig Müller, who was elected Reich bishop in Wittenberg, gave a Nazi salute in front of the town hall door. To honour them, they were escorted by SS men. There are remarkable pictures from this period recording the Hitlerian salute by these men who claimed to be Christians. Faber stated that the Jew was 'without honour, miserly and shameless, compared to the upright character of the German people'.

A little earlier in the year one of the first concentration camps in Germany had been established not far from Wittenberg, in Lichtenberg Castle near Prettin. Many communists and social-democrat Members of Parliament were imprisoned there. Following this, members of Jehovah's Witnesses, Sinti and Roma communities, and homosexuals were imprisoned. These prisoners were then forced to build the Buchenwald concentration camp. By 1939, 1,415 women were imprisoned there. They were then transferred to the Ravensbrück concentration camp.

With the Nazis in power by 1933, severe restrictions were placed on Jews. Fritz, Paul and Kaethe's youngest son, was not allowed to continue with his studies after completing school. Paul bought a farm for him in Wittenberg – in Schatzungsstraße – and Paul would spend time there himself taking on a second role as a farmer.

Further restrictions were now put on the family.[2] One of the most disruptive was the threat to remove Paul from his post in 1933. Dr Otto Emil Rasch was a colleague of the Wittenberg town mayor and became mayor himself for a year in 1935, before having to give this up because of dubious financial dealings involving a villa he was building. He went on to pursue a career in the SS, rising to become head of the Gestapo in Frankfurt in 1938

Fritz, who could not continue his studies because of his half Jewish lineage

and the head of the secret police in Königsberg after that.

He was also involved in the German plot to attack Poland on 31 August 1939. With Reinhard Heydrich, he established the Soldau camp with the aim of murdering Jews and others. Under his authority, 33,771 Jews from Kiev were killed on 29 and 30 September 1941. At the end of the war he was arrested as a war criminal, but managed to avoid punishment because of illness. He died in 1948. In Wittenberg he did his utmost to dismiss Paul Bosse from the hospital. One excuse used was that Paul had been declared disabled after the First Word War. The real reason, of course, was that he had married a girl of Jewish descent. The Nazis were influential in the church, which also ran the hospital, so no favour could be expected from that direction. The fact that Paul Bosse had led the hospital successfully for 14 years was not a consideration.

As the 1930s progressed, the anti-Jewish activities of the Nazis in Wittenberg intensified. The freedom of its Jewish inhabitants was systematically curtailed. It was of no concern whether they were practising their religion or not, or whether they had converted to Christianity, nor did it matter if they were full Jews or half-Jews, or less than that.

A typed list was drawn up of Jewish businesses to be avoided.

Above the names of the businesses on the list was written, 'The Jews are our misfortune. Always remember this. Therefore avoid Jewish businesses.'

Among the names on the list was Hans Ledien, a lawyer, Kaethe Bosse's brother, and also Maier Bosse, a doctor, who was Dolly, the daughter of Paul and Kaethe, and Kate's sister. Neither, as we have seen, professed the Jewish religion.

By 1934 it was only with considerable difficulty that Dolly could continue to practise as a doctor, and then only privately. She was fortunate that she had qualified as a doctor before the Nazi laws prohibited those of mixed race from being doctors. Georg, Dolly's husband (and also known as Schorsch), also faced restrictions as he was taken off the list of teacher assessors.

The day-to-day life of those of Jewish extraction was being severely restricted. They could not continue with their education, and children of German extraction were not to befriend them.

There is evidence that around 15 Wittenberg Jews left the country between 1933 and 1934, including eight shopkeepers. Four went to Palestine, two to the Soviet Union, one to Poland and one to Romania, while the destination of remainder is not known.

Some Jews were imprisoned for befriending German girls. The local newspaper, *Wittenberger Tageblatt*, 20 August 1935, mentions Robert Wiener, a shoemaker, who was 'imprisoned and taken to Lichtenburg Camp, for not having permission to befriend a German girl in his factory'.

Günther had attended the *Melanchthongymnasium* in Wittenberg until 1932, and from there had gone on to study medicine in Munich. He applied to join the International Student Club, but was turned down, as this was a club for Germans according to a rejection letter written on 24 November 1934.

Günther then faced further difficulties. One of the least

significant perhaps, but one which illustrates the restrictions on Jews, was being banned from Wittenberg tennis club. Edith, his wife, was allowed to remain a member. Such letters finish with the usual greeting, 'Heil Hitler!'.

More serious was the refusal of Günther's application to become a doctor after he had passed his examinations in December 1937. On 10 September 1939, in a letter which refers to: sector 3, no. 7, the Reich doctors' organisation, 13 December 1935 (RGB1. I S.1433), he was informed that he would not be recognised as a doctor. When he asked how his sister, of the same descent, had been accepted, he was told that she had already been admitted in 1934, before the law of 13 December 1935. He was allowed to work as a medical practitioner rather than a doctor, and spent some time at St Joseph's Spital in Koblenz, and later served as medical officer at his father's clinic, as he could not use the title of 'doctor'.

The Nazi system required people to trace their ancestry back six generations, in order to find if there was Jewish blood in families. The family tree was kept in a book similar to a passport, called the *Ahnenpass*, or Ancestry Document. The *Ahnenpass* of Paul Bosse and Günther shows that Paul's ancestry was pure enough for the authorities, and that the family could be traced to the beginning of the 18th century. Paul succeeded in finding that one of his forefathers had been a thatcher in Bavaria in the 17th century. The case of Kaethe Bosse, of course, was different, as she had a Jewish background on both sides of the family.

Georg Maier, Dolly's husband, then went on to qualify as a dentist, but he was refused permission to practise. It took him 18 months to win that right, but attempts were still made to make it difficult for him.

Judengeschäfte

Hirschfeldt, Rich., Herrenbekleidungsgeschäft,	Collegienstr. 22
Fuhrmann, Strumpfwaren, Trikotagen,	Markt 6
J. Jsrael, Herrenbekleidung,	Collegienstr. 6
Dr. Gold, Zahnarzt,	Collegienstr. 85
	(bereits ausgebür
Ledien, Hans, Rechtsanwalt,	Coswigerstr. 20
Seligmann, Schuhgeschäft,	Mittelstr. 16 Hof
Gebr. Wiener, Schuhwaren,	Arsenalplatz
E. Bendheim Nachf. Inh. Baumann,	Markt 25
Georg Reimann i. Firma Wollschläger Nachf.	Lutherstr. 29
Maier-Bosse, Ärztin	Kurfürstenstr. 5?

A leaflet urging Germans to avoid Jewish businesses

DEUTSCH-AUSLÄNDISCHER STUDENTENKLUB MÜNCHEN
INTERNATIONAL STUDENT-CLUB MUNICH
Korrespondierendes Mitglied d. Weltstudentenwerkes Genf
GESCHÄFTSSTELLE: MÜNCHEN, LUISENSTR. 67/II (STUDENTENHAUS)
Telephon 55491 · Sprechstunden: jeden Werktag von 11–13 Uhr

Dr.B/Hf.   München, 24.11.34.

Herrn
Günther B o s s e
cand.med.
M ü n c h e n
Karlsplatz 6/I.

Sehr geehrter Herr Bosse!

      Als Vorstandsmitglied des Internationalen Studenten-
klubs habe ich Ihnen mitzuteilen auf Ihr Schreiben vom 19.ds.Mts.
dass nach den neuen am 13.November 1934 genehmigten Satzungen
des Internationalen Studentenklubs Ihre Aufnahme in den Klub
nicht in Frage kommt. Die Satzungen, die mit dem genannten
Termin in Kraft treten, haben folgenden Passus: ---"Förderndes
Mitglied kann jeder Deutsche Studierende werden mit Zustimmung
des Vertreters der Deutschen Studentenschaft.....". Als Ver-
treter der Deutschen Studentenschaft versage ich Ihnen im Ein-
verständnis mit den ausländischen Vorstandsmitgliedern den
Erwerb der Mitgliedschaft des Internationalen Studentenklubs.

                Mit studentischem Gruss !

Anlage:
1 Lichtbild zurück.

Fotokopians överensstämmelse
med originalet intygas:

A letter refusing Günther's application to join a student society

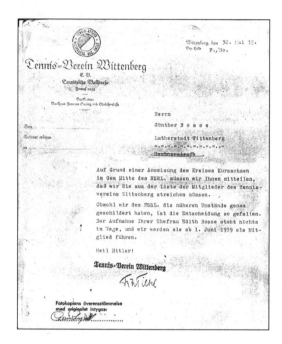

A letter from the
Wittenberg tennis
club ending Günther's
membership

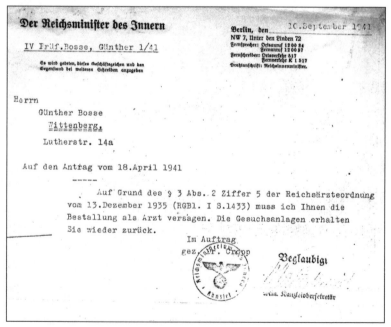

A letter prohibiting Günther from being recognised as a doctor

Paul Bosse's ancestry book

Explosion: Dismissal and Establishing a Clinic

On the afternoon of 13 June 1935, a cloud of smoke rose above the village of Reinsdorf, which could be seen miles away. The people of Wittenberg were worried. Emergency services vehicles could be heard racing towards Reinsdorf. Paul Bosse did not know at the time that the explosion in the munitions factory in Reinsdorf would be a turning point for him, which could also offer him and his family some abatement from Nazi persecution.

The WASAG Company had a large munitions factory in Reinsdorf, around a mile from Wittenberg, employing hundreds of people. The full name of the company was *Westfälisch-Anhaltische Sprengstoff-Actien-Gesellschaft Chemische Fabriken*. It was established in 1891 by Dr Max Bielefeldt, an explosives' chemist, to produce safe explosives for coal mining. It is of interest that this company is still flourishing like so many larger German companies which profited from serving the arms industry, with many of them taking advantage of cheap labour supplied by those in the concentration camps. This company's factories were occupied by the Allies at the end of the Second World War, but as most were located in East Germany, they came under Soviet rule. By now this company has changed its name to H&R WASAG and has 22 factories spread across Germany.

It seems that 120 were killed in the explosion.[3] One source notes that 82 workers were killed, another 112 were seriously injured and 713 suffered lesser injuries.[4] Around 10 million Reichmarks of damage was caused.

The fire lasted for hours according to the report in *Time* magazine on 24 June 1935:

> One afternoon last week peasants miles away from Wittenberg heard a dull roar like distant thunder, followed by other roars which came closer & closer. A huge cloud of reeking yellow smoke mushroomed up from Reinsdorf. In less than a minute, bells were ringing, sirens screaming all over the countryside. Truckloads of soldiers, storm troopers, police, and labor service units were mobilised to keep order. Private automobiles were commandeered to carry dead and wounded. It did not take the shattered windows, the bits of blackened debris dropping from the sky, to tell what had happened: the West-phalian Anhalt munitions works were blowing up.
>
> For nearly seven hours the Sprengstoff continued to explode. Every explosion caused a new fire, every fire a new explosion. Telephone connections were cut off and iron-clad censorship clamped on all news dispatches. Secret police reached the scene almost as quickly as the ambulances, closeted foreign correspondents who attempted to gather first-hand news.

The press reporter thought that around 1,000 had been killed, but this was far from the truth.

The explosion received attention in the international press, including the *Palestine Post*, a volume of whose front pages I came across in a Swansea bookshop many years ago.

That same afternoon, it seems that Paul was at work in the

Toll in German Arms Explosion Reaches 50

Early Reports Exaggerated

NATION PLUNGED INTO MOURNING

(From Reuter)

BERLIN, June 14. — The fear that hundreds of employees were killed in explosion in the Westphal. ian Anhalt explosive works at Reinsdorf, three miles away from Wittenberg, appear to be unfounded, according to official reports. Only 50 dead, 73 seriously injured, and 300 slightly so, are given.

It seems that of the 300 working in the factory at the time, 200 were accounted for after a systematic search, while many inhabitants in the district fled after the first explosion and so escaped further outbreaks. The last of these, at 8 o'clock on Thursday night, sent bricks and parts of machinery flying over an area of three miles.

Factory Wholly Wrecked

Earlier reports of the deathroll had ranged between 500 and 1,500, and the explosion was said completely to have wrecked the factory, which was the biggest and most modern in Germany, employing about 13,000 people.

The first explosion, the cause of which has not yet been established, occurred at 3 o'clock, and was followed by fire and other explosions. The flames of the burning workshops were visible for many miles.

Police and storm troopers cordoned off the district, preventing even the relatives of victims from entering. The press was strictly forbidden to mention the disaster before the publication of the official report.

Paul-Gerhardt-Stift. In a personal report,[5] Dr Kurt Jonas, who followed Paul to lead the Klinik Bosse after the war, said that many Wittenberg citizens had fled to the fields of the Elbe floodplain, fearing more explosions.

Paul arranged that all of the hospital's resources were available immediately to treat the injured who were carried there by the dozen. He spent the next weeks striving to ensure the survival of the injured, and if he already had a good reputation for his work, this earned him even more praise.

The explosion was a national disaster and was a setback to the arms race, with Hitler worried about its effects. Nine days after the event, he came to Wittenberg to visit the injured, to show support for doctors and to gain publicity for himself. Dr Jonas described this visit, 'He [Paul Bosse] had led this criminal rat snatcher from Braunau through the Paul-Gerhardt-Stift, and when he was asked if he had a wish, he asked if it could be ensured that no great misfortune would come to him in view of his marriage to a Jewess. This assurance was given to him, but these were empty words.'

A picture of the event was taken by the local press, showing Hitler shaking the hand of one of the patients, with Paul Bosse at his side.[6]

During his visit to Wittenberg, when he attended the funeral of some of the workers who had been killed, Hitler led a procession through the town's main street. Two little boys looked on. They were firm friends, although they had by now lost this right, as one was a Jew and the other a German. When he came upon the children, Hitler approached one of them and put his hand on his head, saying, 'You have the looks of a perfect little Aryan.' Hitler was not told that this boy was the Jew.[7]

In a report on his work in the hospital during this period, Paul Bosse said after the war:

As senior doctor of the Paul-Gerhardt-Stift I could use new methods I had discovered in treating all the patients and this succeeded in ensuring their survival during the first 24 hours and then in keeping them alive, leading to swift recovery of health. I received the Second Category of the Red Cross, I already had the Third Category.[8]

Only one of the seriously injured workers died. But if Paul had hoped that he and his family would be left in peace by the local Nazis, he was to be disappointed. He was dismissed from his position on 31 December 1935, on the order of the local Nazi authorities, having already received a notice to leave his post on 28 December 1933, because he was not willing to divorce his wife. As it has been noted, the church had a role in issuing this order, as

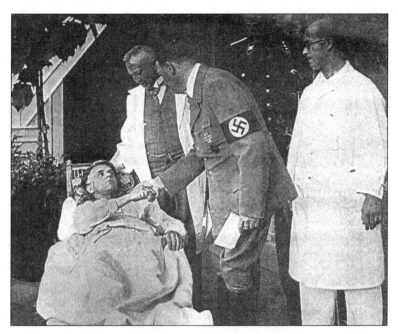

Hitler visiting the hospital after the accident. Paul Bosse stands between him and the patient.

the hospital was run under its sponsorship. Leading church figures were prominent Nazis, and the church was a comfortable player in the Nazi system. Another surgeon, Dr Korth, was one of these leading Nazis, and was associated with the SS. It was he who took Paul's place as the senior doctor of the hospital, although he had no qualifications in gynaecology, as Paul had. Paul mentioned this in his report:

> In spite of my engagement with medical activities, I was further
> persecuted by the Party, the Gestapo, specifically through Dr
> Korth. In the wake of the explosives accident, Hitler, Himmler,
> Goebbels, Ley and others came to the hospital where I was senior
> doctor. I had to take these around and as each one arrived and
> left I shook their hands. During Hitler's visit, many pictures were
> taken, as is usual, and my picture and that of other doctors, with
> patients in them as well.

Paul wrote a letter to Joseph Goebbels complaining that he had been dismissed because of his wife's 'non-Aryan' descent, but no reply was received to refute his claim.

> Medical report on the explosives accident in Reinsdorf.
> Herrn Reichsminister Dr. Göbbels, Berlin.
> Urgent. Personal.
>
> Following my oral report which I gave personally on the 14.VI to the Herrn Reichsminister, I would like to add the following, to clarify the situation:
> In total at the Paul-Gerhardt-Stift in Wittenberg, 93 injured people were received to be treated at the hospital, 33 of them with broken arms or legs, 26 with head injuries, 8 with serious burns, and 57 with wounds to the face and body. All those wounded were treated with a German preparation... For anaesthetic it was possible to operate without chloroform and ether, by using a German vaccination preparation, which put the patients under anaesthetic for between 10 and 20 minutes, and then woke them up without side-effects and without requiring additional staff, and so this method would be an appropriate choice for cases of mass injuries and for war purposes...

The letter went on to give the details of some of the patients and how they were treated, and also mentions 200 other patients who were treated as outpatients. Then the letter states:

> I don't know whether the Herr Reichsminister has been told through Herr Reidenreich that the church board has ended my post as senior doctor at the Paul-Gerhardt-Stift on 31.XII, although I had been working there for 28 years, had fought at the front in the war and had been injured, because my wife, with whom I have been married since 1906, is of non-Aryan descent. In appreciation of the large number of my wife's family who fell in the war, my eldest daughter was accepted as a doctor in 1934. I have attached the vote by the Board, although this is very difficult for me, as I have built the hospital up from the smallest beginnings. I do not know whether some in the Nazi state wanted to remove me from this post.

We have all suffered under the shattering experience of the serious misfortune that struck our fatherland. I have done my duty, of course, without expecting a word of thanks from the institution's clergy. I was however extremely surprised when, instead of that, an institution clergyman, Priest Stosch, asked me if I wanted to give up the post earlier. I cannot consider such a question... but as an attack on my work. Otherwise I would not have turned to the Herr Reichsminister in connection to the national misfortune. This event, however, forces me to ask the Herr Reichsminister whether the Nazi state, which I serve faithfully, has taken issue against me in this situation and whether I am to be released from entitlement to hold a post. Heil Hitler![9]

Facing being dismissed from his post, he set about establishing a *Privatklinik und Entbindungsanstalt* – a private hospital/clinic and maternity hospital – in his home, at his own cost, and he met with success. He extended the home and opened the small new hospital in 1936.

At the beginning he was helped by two nurses, one was an independent nurse, and the other belonged to the Wittenberg Catholic community. Paul Bosse also had connections with the Order of *Marienschwestern* – sisters of Maria – through a local Catholic priest, and he asked for their help. On 1 March 1936 the first of the *Marienschwestern* came to the clinic, and the second came on 7 April. Later a community of Catholic nuns ran the hospital. These were part of the *Institut der Schönstätter Marienschwestern*, which belonged to the international family of Schönstatt. It was to Paul Bosse's advantage that the main hospital had no birth specialist, and the Klinik Bosse soon became popular. The family moved to the top floor of the building, a substantial attic, in July 1936 to make room for the hospital. By December four Maria sisters were working there, and the family moved to Thälmannstraße, named after Ernst Thälmann, leader of the Communist Party during the period of the Weimar

Republic. In 1933 he was arrested by the Gestapo, and in 1944, having been kept in solitary confinement, he was shot on Hitler's orders. When the family moved to this street, the name had been changed to Adolf Hitler Straße. The nurses were then free to take over the attic. The kitchen was above the garage, a step or two higher than the level of the lower wards. A larger kitchen needed to be built, and a new bathroom to accommodate the ten sisters who were working in the clinic by 1940. In 1939 one room was refurbished as a chapel, and the first mass was held there on 25 March 1939. Dr Jonas's report mentions that Paul Bosse was 'skilful and experienced, well-known in Wittenberg and well-liked by the people'.

In the wake of his success, the authorities tried to prohibit the clinic from receiving contributions from the sickness fund which paid for patients' treatment. A decision was made – probably by local Nazis – that the new clinic should not receive insurance funds. A hearing was held in the main insurance office in Merseburg, which was responsible for deciding which institutions could receive patients' insurance money in order to provide medical treatment. The office wrote to Paul Bosse on 14 March 1936 to overturn the local decision. On the basis of the Nuremberg Laws, there was a detailed definition of 'Jewish doctors' and the office noted this in its judgement:

> Full Jews with four Jewish grandparents, threequarter-Jews with three grandparents of Jewish descent and those half-Jews with two Jewish grandparents, who on 16 September 1935 belonged to the Jewish religious community or who had been accepted after that, or who at the same time were married to a Jew or had married a Jew after that. All other doctors are considered to be non-Jewish, also mixed Jews (half and quarter-Jews) and the non-Jewish doctors who married a Jew.

There is another paragraph with similar phraseology noting which patients Jewish and non-Jewish doctors could accept. The

The family home in Wittenberg before it was transformed as a clinic

conclusion was that 'Herr Dr Bosse and his daughter are not "Jewish" doctors, and so there is no reason to prohibit the clinic to members of the insurance scheme and to others who belong to them.'

One of the restrictions placed on the family was that Paul's wife, Kaethe, would not be allowed to work in the clinic, nor to live there, and this made matters difficult. Dr Jonas notes that Kaethe was a 'pleasant, dear and kind' lady, who suffered especially when she realised that she was the cause of the persecution. She came close to taking her own life, he said.

Kaethe would later tend the land owned by the family, and grew produce that would give mothers who came to the clinic the best nourishment. For the time being the family were free from arrest, and Kaethe's forced absence from the clinic meant that the town's German population were not prohibited from attending.

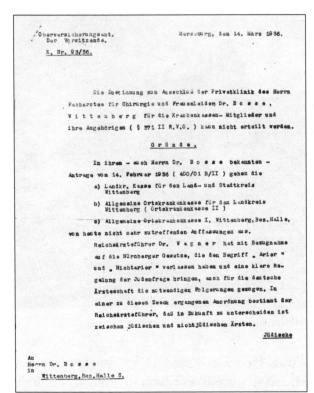

The first page of the insurance office letter allowing Paul Bosse to act as a non-Jewish doctor, and to receive non-Jewish patients

The picture of Paul Bosse and Hitler was to be seen on the new clinic's wall in an attempt, possibly, to show that Paul's work was approved of, and as an indication that any attempt by local Nazis to harm the clinic would be in some way an insult to the Führer. By the end of 1936 therefore, it seemed to the Wittenberg public that Paul had succeeded in guaranteeing his family's safety from Nazi persecution, and a part of this success was his work following the explosion in Reinsdorf.

Attacks against those who had married Jews were becoming more and more intolerable, according to Dr Jonas. In spite of this, many people who had been coerced into becoming Nazis were sending their wives to the clinic for childbirth, but were doing so secretly. The authorities still wanted to boycott the clinic. When *Kristallnacht* occurred, the night arranged by the Nazis for lawless gangs to attack Jewish property, a crowd of local vandals attacked the home of Hans Ledien, Kaethe's brother, and then a cry arose, 'Jetzt zu Bosse!' ['Now for Bosse']. Someone warned the clinic and, in fear, the family waited for the threatened attack. Fortunately, it did not materialise.

Nazism in Wittenberg continued to escalate. A supplement of the *Wittenberger Tageblatt* for 9–13 September 1933 included an article by the Chief-inspector of churches in the Wittenberg area, Professor Maximilian Meichßner, in which he considered that a 'Führer' was called by God. On the 390th anniversary of Luther's death in 1936, Professor Maximilian Meichßner reiterated without criticism Luther's hatred of the Jews, in a sermon preached in the *Stadtkirche*. (Unfortunately his later rejection of Nazi ideology and criminal actions came too late for Wittenberg's Jews. His son, Joachim, was executed for his part in the plot of 20 July 1944 to assassinate Hitler, and he was imprisoned for five months.)

In May 1937 the street called Jüdenstraße [Jewish street] was changed to Wettinerstraße, replacing the reference to Jews with a reference to the German princely community. Searches were also made in works and factories to discover whether they were Jewish-owned or not.

Adverts appeared in the local press denouncing Jews, on the basis that they were responsible for crucifying Jesus, without acknowledging that Jesus was a Jew. An exhibition, 'Blood and Race', was held at Melanchthon Grammar School, Wittenberg, at the beginning of April 1937, and a series of anti-Jewish articles was published in local papers. Luther was praised as the greatest revolutionary of his age by Gauleiter Joachim Eggeling, the Nazi leader for Saxony and Anhalt, and the Nazi ideologist,

The maternity
section of the
Klinik Bosse at
Heubnerstraße

The clinic staff
preparing
food

Dr Kurt Jonas,
Paul Bosse's
successor
in the Klinik
Bosse, with
Schwester
Simone and
Schwester
Gaudentia,
one of the
nuns who
worked with
Paul Bosse

Paul and Kaethe Bosse,
around 1940

Reichsleiter Alfred Rosenberg, who was later sentenced to death by the Nürnberg trials. In March 1938 the town name was changed to include Luther's name. From now on it would be known as Wittenberg-Lutherstadt.

At the end of 1936 Kate, now an Egyptologist, lost her position in the museum in Berlin, and was forced to leave the country. She chose England as her destination, with the help of an institution in Paris which communicated with an organisation helping Jews in England.

In the same year the finance office in Magdeburg suggested that Paul Bosse should emigrate. He considered South America, among other places, and he had to pay emigration taxes to the Reich, which was tantamount to property theft. Other emigration possibilities were considered continually by the family. In a letter to her daughter Kate on 8 December, Kaethe wrote, 'Karl Henschel, Mexico, a friend from his younger days, and who has supported Opa, has invited him by telegraph to go to America.'

In 1938 Kaethe's property was possessed, and she had to pay

a quarter of its value to reclaim it. The same year, Hans Ledien, her brother, who worked as a lawyer, was arrested and taken to Buchenwald concentration camp.

There were other restrictions on the family's freedom: they had no right to go to the cinema, and no right to listen to the radio as it was confiscated.

In April 1944 the authorities attempted to persuade Paul Bosse to close the clinic and tried to force him to do military service. A month later, an attempt was made to force his son Fritz to leave the farm and take him to a camp, but although these efforts were resisted, the family was now under great pressure.

Eva: the army officer's wife

A T THE SAME TIME as these events were taking place in Wittenberg, the effects of persecution were felt even more deeply by Eva, Kaethe's sister.

Eva was married to Willibald Borowietz, an army officer. His army career began on 5 March 1914. He was injured twice in the First World War, and left the army in 1920 to join the police in Breslau (Wroclaw today), becoming a major there. He rejoined the army towards the end of 1935. He had many posts in the army and rose swiftly in the ranks to become a major in the same year.[10] By the end of 1938 the Nuremberg Laws were being stringently applied. No Jew was to hold a public post, and people married to those of Jewish descent were also restricted.

This ruling hit Willibald Borowietz's family hard. Williband and Eva had three children, Joachim, Wilma and Eva Monika. It seems that Willibald had been told that he would have no hope of promotion and could be dismissed if he remained married to Eva. On the other hand, if he divorced his wife, his children would be considered as Aryan.

One afternoon in October 1938, when Eva Monika, who was then 14, returned home from school near Berlin, she found her mother hanged. Throughout her life Eva's view was that her mother had sacrificed her life for the sake of her family in the hope that the others would survive. There is no greater sacrifice. Her hope was partly realised. The children lived and became Aryan.

Eva Ledien and Willibald Borowietz

Eva (Ledien) Borowietz, with two of her children around 1925

However, during the first weeks of the Second World War, her son, Joachim, was burnt to death in a tank.

Among the family papers, there is a letter written by Willibald Borowietz to the army authorities offering his resignation at the end of the year, giving the injuries received in the First World War as grounds for his request. The letter was dated on the day of his wife's suicide. One can only imagine the circumstances at home on that fateful day. Recently in a search of army archives, my cousin Ute and her husband Detlev came across a letter from the army authorities accepting the resignation. As matters then transpired, Willibald Borowietz kept his position and became an *Oberstleutnant* yn 1940.

For the rest of her life Eva Monika would be filled with hate at the sight of images of Hitler. When television programmes would be broadcast about Hitler's life, even 50 years after the war, she would feel an urge to smash the television set, just as Hitler and his cronies had destroyed her family.

Eva Borowietz's funeral service was held at a crematorium in Wilmersorf, Berlin. Many army officers were present to pay their respects to one who had sacrificed her life for a fellow officer.

By now Kate was in England. Her mother Kaethe found it difficult to communicate the news of Eva's demise to her daughter. This is the text of her letter:

27 October 1938

My dear Katrinchen,

Knubben [the family pet name for Edith, Günther's wife] was very happy to receive your lovely card. Tante Mulzer wanted to come on Saturday, to have more advice. My dearest, I have to write today unfortunately that our Tante Eva has lost her nerve, or in a completely erroneous spirit of not wanting to stand in her husband's way, has chosen early death – I am so sad that she did not, as she would do in the past, manage to visit us often. Opa can always give good advice. Will [Willibald, Eva's husband] is

Eva Monika, one of Eva
Ledien's two daughters

Am 26. Oktober 1938 entriß uns ein jäher Tod meine geliebte Frau, die gute

Mutter unserer Kinder

Frau Eva Borowietz
geb. Ledien.

Sie wird uns immer ein Vorbild sein.

Namens aller Hinterbliebenen

Willibald Borowietz

Major (E)
im Kommando der Panzertruppenschule

Berlin-Tempelhof, den 27. Oktober 1938
Burgherrenstr. 2.

Die Trauerfeier findet am Montag, dem 31. Oktober, 14 Uhr, im Krematorium Berlin-
Wilmersdorf, Berliner Str. 100, statt.
Es wird gebeten, von Beileidsbesuchen Abstand zu nehmen.

The funeral leaflet of
Eva Borowietz

weeping and unhappy and yet I don't believe that he gave her proper support. We had already discussed this. There will never again be an officer's wife as gentle and as brave as our little Eva. I remember how at Christmas she would go about everything with so much energy…

Dear Katrinchen, Now I must be able to write a happy letter once again. I must write everything to you, happy things and other things. A kiss from your mother.

The funeral was a painful affair. In a letter on 1 November 1938, Paul wrote to his daughter Kate:

My dear Katrinchen,

Yesterday Eva was put to rest in the crematorium in Wilmersdorf. Many officers and their wives came, including the General, to pay their last respects to her and they had flowers and wreaths to a brave officer's wife who will not be forgotten. Will was proud, his application had been stopped and tomorrow he can apply for promotion. For the first time I wore my medals publicly as a show – *you know why*. Following that we had coffee and cake together.

We soon travelled home. Yes, yes, you know your father and believe me, I did not have much peace tonight. They have already arranged a housekeeper for the children, and everything is working like clockwork.

Paul clearly wanted to make an impression in front of the army officers by displaying the medals he had won for bravery in the First World War. This, he hoped, would be a further sign of his faithfulness to the current order, but his motive, of course, was to defend his family from further persecution. His scorn towards Willibald is clear, in that he saw that he had lost no time in making arrangements for another woman to care for his children so that he would be free to renew his army career.

At the end of her husband's letter, Kaethe adds:

Dearest,

Yesterday was almost worse that Eva's death. I have never experienced anything so revolting, and I'm afraid that the children will soon face a bitter end. I can send you today at last the garment that Frau Aster had not finished,

From my heart,

Mutti

Soon her brother Hans would be taken to Buchenwald, and with her sister having committed suicide, Kaethe's worry for the fate of her sister's children was understandable. The Nazi persecution of Jews had brought death to the family, and it would not be easy to escape the clutches of the Nazi system.

Kaethe's opinion of Willibald Borowietz is clear in a letter written on 8 December 1938, where she notes his title scornfully, and compares him unfavourable with the husband of Erika, her sister-in-law:

My dear daughter,

Your lovely letter has arrived. I have just been with Erika, who has been living in her flat since yesterday. Her husband, who is a quite excellent man, lives with her. It has done her a lot of good that you've shown so much care for her. Herr Major Borowietz is quite the opposite and did not manage to go to the Consulate with his children to look after them.

Willibald Borowietz inspecting soldiers on the Theresienwiese, Munich, where the Oktoberfest is held today

As it happened, Willibald was further promoted during the war, becoming *Oberst* in 1942, *Generalmajor* on 1 January 1943, and then *Generalleutnant* on 1 May 1943.

During the war he became commander of the 50th Anti-tank Battalion, he led the 10th Rifle Regiment, and then led and commanded Rommel's 15th Tank (*Panzer*) Division at the beginning of 1943. In this post he served under the Generalfeldmarschall Erwin Rommel in the battle of Kasserine Pass, Tunisia. This tank division had been defeated when German forces were shattered in North Africa on 13 May 1943. It is said that the tanks went into their last battle with Tunisian wine as petrol, as no other fuel was available. Willibald discussed the terms of surrender to American forces with two other generals.[11] He had won a host of medals, including the Knight's Iron Cross and Oak Leaves, the highest honour, but after surrender to the Americans he went, in the first instance, as a prisoner to an American camp in Britain.

He wrote letters to Frau Annemarie Limbacher, who looked after his two daughters, Eva Monika and Wilma, although another family was their legal guardian. On 24 May 1943 he wrote to her:

> My daughters must have told you about my misfortune, my imprisonment. My fate was to be taken prisoner when I was with the regiment of which my son was a member when he was killed. We did not lose our honour! … I'm healthy and I am treated correctly. I ask you to be good enough to write to my daughters and to help them. You can write to me as often as you wish… Let my girls know about the contents of this letter.

By June 1943 he had been taken to a prisoner of war camp in America. He wrote again many times, and by 19 July, he was in a camp in Texas:

> After a train journey of four days we came to our camp of barracks, which is treeless, ten days ago… We are in good spirits and in

good health. How are my girls? Eva–Monika must be on holidays now? Everyday life here is very monotonous, without German books, sports equipment that has been damaged, but the company is good.

On 16 December, Willibald is somewhat worried about Eva Monika – she and her sister Wilma were now in the care of Annemarie and her husband in Gemünden am Main:

I appreciate greatly that you are willing to take Wilma my eldest daughter as well. This relieves my heart from a heavy burden. But I have to ask you again to ensure that Eva-Monika finishes her course in the secondary school, that the two girls remain in Gemünden, and rent a room together, unless they have to go to do *Arbeitsdienst* [work service] or do other charity work connected to the war. They should not become a burden to you.

On 16 March 1944, Willibald wrote to Eva Monika in Gemünden stating that the Limbacher family were now her official guardians. There was apparently some disagreement with the family in Berlin who had fulfilled this role until now:

In everything that you do, remember the family's reputation, and whether your mother would approve… I'm fine, and have had an excellent book from Frau Limbacher on Friedrich der Große. Love, your father.

He sent a letter to Frau Limbacher on 11 May 1944 and mentioned that he was having his artificial eye replaced. This letter shows his confidence, but on 11 May he is worrying again about the disagreement between Wilma and the family in Berlin. In another letter he asks Frau Limbacher to ensure that his girls receive sums of money, and keeps an account of their spending.

His commitment to the war continued, despite the passing months of his imprisonment. The conditions, however, were very different from those in German camps, and he was free to write as he wished and to receive letters and gifts. He said on 12 August 1944:

It's better for you and the girls to remember me as I was at home. As I know well the area where you live, I can imagine everything that you're writing about. My thoughts and good wishes are with you as you bear the heavy burden of war. May God give you strength. My daughters should do war work, that is important and necessary. Studies and personal life can wait. Only when Germany lives can we live.

By now Willibald was prisoner in Clinton camp, Mississippi. He heard that his daughter Wilma was about to marry an army officer. He wrote on 11 November 1944:

If it is true, give her my best wishes. It won't be easy for them, as he is an officer on duty, and the two have nothing. Just as when Eva and I married, a typical officer pair. But we were so happy although the time was short. Best wishes to Hohensee [Wilma's betrothed], that he soon recovers from his wounds. It must be nice for Wilma to know at least that he is in Germany.

A letter on 16 December 1944 discusses the financial details of marriage:

I am in complete agreement with Wilma's engagement, and a long engagement would be ridiculous. After the war she will receive a payment of around RM1000, and an additional RM200 a month after marrying. This will make life a little easier, especially when combined with her husband's income. My wish is that she stops studying after getting married, if this is possible with the war still on. I'm asking you and your husband to represent me at the wedding…

However, within seven months, Willibald Borowietz was dead. According to one family story he was killed by electrical equipment – an accident according to some, suicide according to others.[12] There is nothing in the letters to suggest a mental illness that would lead to suicide. He expresses concern for his family in Germany, and there are also some positive plans. Having said that, by July 1945, it was clear that it was all over for Hitler. Did Willibald lose the will to live, with Germany collapsing, and his life in tatters? There is another report suggesting that he was killed in a road accident.[13] He was buried in Fort Bennig, the highest-ranking German officer to be buried there, and his two daughters were now orphans.

Hans Ledien escapes

GRADUALLY THE JEWS WERE squeezed out of various aspects of the town's life: their businesses were possessed, they were driven from the town, and then came the evening of *Kristallnacht*, 9 November 1938. By then there were no more than 50 Jews in the town. In spite of this, the eve of Martin Luther's birthday was chosen to attack the property, houses and businesses of those Jews who remained. Wreckage was caused and synagogues burnt.

The destruction was arranged on a national level. Locally, SS officers had arranged gangs, including the dregs of society, to do the work. In Wittenberg two groups of local people came together for the attack on businesses.

By the time her brother Günther wrote the following letter to Kate, he had gone to Sweden, and what he had witnessed in Wittenberg had left an indelible impression on him. Hans, his mother's brother, was the family member who suffered most during those days: his property was broken into, and as he was then taken to Buchenwald. His daughter, Erika, was forced to watch the attack.

27.12.1938, from Karlshamn, Sweden
Thank God that we could travel to Sweden – at one time it appeared that my passport would not be extended – I have no joys to report. I suppose that you can recreate most of what happened from newspaper reports. Things started with Eva's death. She took her own life, otherwise Will would have had to have left his position on the 1st of January. Already Jewish doctors had to leave their work on 1 October, and lawyers on 30 November. The police had gone to Hans to ask him if he wished to emigrate and

so on. The shock to Oma was enormous. Oma tried to kill herself several times, to lesser and greater degrees of intent, sometimes with gas, sometimes with sleeping medicine, which of course would scarcely be effective in Oma's case. We were all enormously worried and rarely did we leave Oma on her own.

Dolly could not look after her at all as she has still not recovered. Her illness must be psychological to a large extent – too much work and financial worries. She has too many debts – the facilities at her clinic are excellent but insanely large, and Schorch [Georg, Dolly's husband] has destroyed a large part of his practice, as he travelled to Yugoslavia. But that will sort itself out again and we're doing everything to give Dolly a month or two in a sanatorium. But at the moment she is not a help but a burden. (Her children, conversely, are pure pleasure.)

But then came the murder in Paris.[14] You probably know everything about the laws that followed that. People in rage (riff-raff organised by anonymous SS leaders) have caused about a hundred million Marks' worth of damage. The two days were horrid. A loaded revolver lay all the time on Opa's writing desk. Matters were soon at hand in Wittenberg: Hans and many other Jews were arrested. Then the police took possession of all weapons. After that the gasworks extinguished the gas and the lights and then came 'the rage'. Working in two groups the flats of wealthy Jews and businesses and offices were demolished. An attack by a bomb would not have caused worse havoc. Erika was forced to watch (and yet in her home they left a comparatively large number of things untouched); four full clothes baskets of porcelain. Among other things they destroyed all the furniture. Then the persecution continued in the papers, on the radio etc. Having said that, it all appeared to be excessive to very many people.

But the results: whoever is in contact with a Jew is, to all intents and purposes, greatly distrusted, and will have one foot already in the concentration camp. A Jew is no longer a man, he has no rights, and emigration is being made difficult. I don't think that newspapers can come near to describing the torture and the vandalism.

Hans was in the concentration camp for five weeks. He was

not allowed to have mail, and he was allowed to write three times. There were 25,000 in the camp from November onwards and 10,000 of them were Jews. He was not allowed to say a word about how they were treated. They threatened to shoot him... He was then told if he did not leave Germany within a few months, he would be taken back into the concentration camp and he would never be released.

They did not sleep in barracks, but, it seems, on the ground under one blanket, had far too little to drink and NO kind of work at all! A man's life is worth nothing there – he survived everything well, better than expected, but in spirit he has almost been destroyed. Oma has somehow recovered, at least she did not suffer personally. And in town people are extremely friendly. It must be said that the authorities are ashamed, at least up to the Gestapo, who are omnipotent.

Those of mixed race are not affected by all this, but things have not got better either.

Opa's nerves have suffered through it all as he has to fear the worst – the worst are the rumours – and the attacks are so often against Opa. But without much success, I think, and I don't think that the clinic will have to suffer much either. Naturally Oma has been kept out of the business completely, and she has to look after the fine new flat. But all this is not easy.

You must write at once about your plans. How long will your money last? How are things with work possibilities? We will try to get money for you here, so that you are continually supported. Or should we also try to find work for you in a city here? I'm sure that with your languages you could find work as a journalist. But answer at once, because it will be difficult, at best, to find something. Because of Hans I'm writing to Mexico to his school friend. The affidavit (or whatever it is called) has still not come. At worst, if everything fails, you must try to see what Hans can do in England. He has until 1.IV.39 before he has to get out of Germany.

Destroy this letter at once please.

Günther

How much money to you want in a month? At the moment everything in Wittenberg is in order. The clinic this year has had almost 700 more patients than last year.

Many attempts were made following this to find refuge for Hans in other countries. There is one letter from Audrey Turner of the *Society of Friends German Emergency Committee* (17 January 1939), a group of Quakers, addressed to a Mrs Ethel Oates of Leeds, regarding getting a British visa for Hans Ledien. It's clear that she had got in touch with the society on behalf of Hans, but the answer was not hopeful:

> In order to obtain a permit for a refugee to enter this country it is necessary either that he should have a post to come to, or that his plans for emigration elsewhere should already have been made.
>
> I am afraid, therefore, it would not be possible for Herr Ledien to come over here upon the offer of a few months' hospitality...

Hans Ledien in 1935

On 19 January 1939, Mrs Oates wrote to Hans Ledien with an offer for him to come to England to teach German to her sons, while he confirmed more concrete arrangements to emigrate to South America:

> Would it be possible for me to extend to you some months of hospitality, when you would talk German to my sons?
>
> I have asked for a visa, and it appears from the supplementary papers that you must accept someone who can undertake work for an unlimited time. I'm not in a position to do that, but if you can give a reference for emigrating to America or details regarding emigrating to somewhere else, or if I can set about finding someone else who could take you as a German teacher.
>
> I hope you can be in a position to take advantage of this offer, and if so I will try to fill the attached form as quickly as possible, so that the Home Ministry gives a visa.

On 22 January 1939 Hans wrote to Kate in England thanking her for her efforts in finding him employment. Hans notes that he has not yet had a visa or an affidavit to travel to North America, nor permission to emigrate to Mexico, and he has not heard either from his friend from Puebla in that country. The difficulty in coming to Britain is because there has been no offer of a permanent post, and he fears that all hope is disappearing.

By 1 February 1939 Hans has strong doubts that he will be able to travel to see Kate in London. He had gone to the office of the Friends' Association in Berlin, but his application was refused. In order to visit England he had to obtain proof that he would only be there for a limited period, and that he had permission to permanently move to another country. He was advised in Berlin to enquire with the German Jewish Aid Committee in London. In the meantime he had an invitation to visit a friend in Verdun, France. There was a further possibility of going to Algeria, and his friend was willing to look into this.

He received kind support from Ronald Gurney of Bristol

University on 25 February, who said that he was willing to give Hans a financial guarantee until he went to America.

By 19 March 1939 Hans hoped to have a visa to travel to Chile but, in the meantime, Chile stopped giving permission to more immigrants.

Hans wrote to Dr Gurney asking him to transfer $200 on his behalf to the Palestine & Orient Lloyd in Paris. He had received advice from a travel office in Leipzig that such arrangements had to be made via a Paris office. During that week, in order to arrange emigration, he had been to Berlin, Magdeburg, twice to Leipzig and then back again to Berlin. By now it seemed that a place was available for him on a ship, and that ship would take him to Shanghai.

Later, Erika, who was a little girl at the time, recorded the experience of *Kristallnacht* at her home, and she added her father's story who had been imprisoned in Buchenwald following an attack on his office and home. She starts with an account of her father leaving Germany for Shanghai.

> My father peeled the apple in such a comical way that I had a large tail of skin, and he cut some nasty looking faces on the skins of the oranges, and he could depict all the characters of the tales. But when he took me on a bike journey to Teucheler woods, he wept. This was his last journey before he flew from Leipzig to Rome, and travelled then from Genua by ship to Shanghai. Mum, Uncle Walter [Walter Mannchen, the husband of Leonore Herzfeld, who was a second cousin to her mother] and I went with Dad to Leipzig. I was given a children's coat from Hamburg and the red hat. Uncle Walter exchanged the briefcase with Dad. Then the plane went smaller and smaller in the sky.
>
> I wished that he didn't suffer from bile and wondered how that would be in Shanghai, where Uncle Paul could not come to give him an injection. So often I would hear the heavy steps around the house when Dad would walk around plagued by pains, and then Uncle Paul's car, Mum and Uncle Paul whispering and Dad

groaning. I would wait quietly in my room in bed. But once I got up, and there were Mum and Uncle Paul, and also Aunty Kaethe and Dad, who was stinking awfully. He had just been released from Buchenwald. He came without a coat; he had left that with a man there who had not yet been released. Dad was thin and pitiful and quiet. He was prohibited from talking about his time in prison. Everyone who was released from prison had sworn to keep quiet. Dad came home to a house that had changed completely. Instead of the three people who were living there, there were more than a dozen now in the house. A Jewish family had been put in almost every room after the *Reichskristallnacht* on 9 November 1938. In the lounge was the young Kühn pair with a baby who was not yet a year old. In the men's room were the old Israel couple, in the living room the widow Klein with her grown-up daughter, in another room the married Hirschfeld couple with twins in their teens. The Hirschfeld family were the only ones that managed to flee. They already had papers for Palestine, and I remember their farewell present, a fountain pen for me.

All the inhabitants were thoroughly frightened, and they could only bring the most essential things from home with them. Some of them had brought temporary beds. They had no contact with the area where they had previously lived and they were sentenced to be without anything to do, because their shops had closed or because they had been banned from their workplaces. They were not allowed to go out of the house, and in front of the house every day we saw men in leather coats. Our old neighbour, Frau Böttcher, would take many litres of milk from the milk cart and would put them – as she had done for months – behind in the garden on the wall for us.

My plaits were practical as I did not have to go to cut my hair. That would have been bad, because after 1938 one had to be prepared to be thrown out of a shop. We did not know the exact rules, but it was clear that no-one after *Kristallnacht* could go to the theatre, cinema, concert or to any exhibition. Our movements were very restricted. It seems that only Jews and not the 'mixed people' suffered this, but no-one had received full information and we always tried to avoid painful situations.

Often we saw that the rules were being administered 150 per cent. For example, I wasn't allowed later to go to the grammar school in Stettin, although there was no rule about this. After 1935 my father had more and more difficulty in carrying out his job and eventually the right to act as a *Notariat* was taken from him, and this was his main source of income. He made applications then to obtain a visa. At first he made attempts to have a visa for France. He had been a student in Grenoble and for a while in Paris, and was very fond of France. But he had no hope of working there. It was the same in the Netherlands and Switzerland. Then my father set his sights on South America, and tried to obtain an affidavit, and travelled regularly to Berlitz in Berlin and learnt Spanish. Everything should have been made quicker by paying a large sum of money, but my father was caught out by a swindler.

He was now regularly torn between plans to emigrate and staying in Germany. But being arrested in November 1938 had brought every consideration to a halt. In October my father's younger sister had killed herself in Berlin. Eva's husband, an officer in the army, was to be thrown out of the army because he was married to a Jewess. After her death he could continue with his career, and even become a general. Aunt Eva's and his children, Jochen, Wilma and Eva-Monika, were accepted as Aryans. Jochen died as a young 19-year-old soldier during the first weeks of the war. My father had an especially close relationship with Eva, and they had a circle of mutual friends in Berlin (where he had met my mother) and as an uncle who was very fond of children he could have seen his nephew and nieces grow up and given them substantial financial help. He had lived until he was 42 with his mother in his parents' spacious home, and there was enough time and room to accommodate the family from Berlin. He was horrified by the death of his sister. Soon afterwards he was arrested in the office and after a few days in Wittenberg's cross-examination prison he was moved to Buchenwald. Frau Walter had taken food to him every day in prison; one day she came back empty-handed: Dad was no longer there.

The night after my father was arrested, hoards of men came to hit our house door and to smash the windows and inside the house everything they could get hold of at the time was strewn everywhere: glass doors, lamps, mirrors, the contents of cupboards. Furnishings were cut open, pictures on the walls were ripped, my doll was destroyed, its sleeping eyes were pushed in and its head completely damaged. The glass cupboard with my father's large collection of tin soldiers had been thrown down, but it wasn't shattered. Some of the contents of the house were missing after *Kristallnacht*, but none of the collection of tin soldiers was lost.

My mother, who was alone in the house with me, could not call for help, the electricity and the phone were not working. We were extremely afraid. We were being chased around the house, it was dark, we stumbled, the men hit us, things were being broken and shattered, there was shouting everywhere...

Then at some point Walter's mother arrived and she took us to her house. For days Mum and Frau Griebel, the old housemaid who would come many times a week on her old bicycle although my parents were no longer allowed to have a maid, cleared up. Shards everywhere, cupboard doors ripped loose, curtains torn, pictures holed... Frau Griebel remained a faithful soul. She often talked about 'her club' (the Communist Party). At home she had her old husband, blind and on his pension, a disabled grandson and a young lodger in her dining room by the kitchen...

After my father was released from Buchenwald in the spring of 1939, at my mother's request as he had been an officer who had won awards in the First World War, the Gestapo would worry us all the time in order to drive my father out of the country. Through an SA man, he obtained passage on a ship from Genua to Shanghai which had been booked by a Jew, but who had died before travelling. The journey was for one person. My mother and I were to travel later, but then the Second World War started on 1 September 1939 and that was not possible. My parents by then had psychological and financial problems.

It seems that it was easier to go to Shanghai than to other places: there was no need for a visa or special permission − a travel ticket was enough. He had a place to stay in the Navy YMCA in Shanghai, but things were difficult enough. He said in a letter to Stina (a cousin of Günther's wife in Sweden) on 2 June 1941 that no-one in Shanghai had asked them to be there, they had not brought any money with them, but they were trying to live and find employment. For his own part, he said that he was fortunate that he had a talent for learning languages, and by living in the YMCA he had an opportunity to practise his English. He also took lessons in Chinese, but he found that language very difficult. Another difficulty was that he was learning Mandarin, the language of the authorities, but not the language spoken by the ordinary people. He mastered enough to use the language in the street and in restaurants, but he said that he needed to learn the language properly in order to discuss business. It was not an easy time to be in Shanghai, because of the war; few ships would call, coal was scarce and light had to be used sparingly. Hans joined the Shanghai special police in November 1941, which was voluntary work, but he would have some food when serving twice a week. By now the Japanese had occupied the YMCA, and he had a place in a French establishment and then in a room in

K.=L. Buchenwald

Ledien Hans .... Häftlings-Nr. 28611

(Vor- und Zuname)

geb. am 20.10.87 zu Middenberg Fahrgeld

Datum	Zugang		Abgang		Bestand		
	RM	Pf	RM	Pf	RM	Pf	
12.11.38	23	13			23	13	Pol.Gef.Halle.
30.11.			23	13	—	—	× Ledien
3.12.	25	—	—	—	25	—	
5.12.38			25	—	—	—	× Ledien
	48	13	48	13	—		Me

A financial register document when Hans Ledien, aged 51, was prisoner at Buchenwald

131 Museum Road, where there were pleasant gardens. He said that his Chinese was getting better, but he could only understand between 800 and 1,000 of the language's characters, and at least around 3,500 were needed to read a paper.

Hans now was writing in English, as this was easier for the censors. He gave an account of his life in Shanghai in a letter to Kate after the war, dated 11 February 1948:

> The years in Shanghai passed by quickly. To start things were very difficult! I had no English, and I didn't see any possibility of being of service. Then things came to order gradually, although I was also starving for a long time. Then the end of 1941 came and in 1942 times got better, but in 1943 the Japanese made things really difficult for us immigrants, as they formed some kind of ghetto. After the end of the Pacific Ocean War things got better. From November 1945 I was the manager of the Business Appliance Company and dealt with typewriters and counting machines and other office equipment, and I could live quite well in the circle of my Chinese employers. I learnt English well and Chinese fairly well and have a lot of sympathy for the Chinese. A bitter time came in my struggle to try to come home. Only on 25 July did I manage to leave Shanghai and at last I was back on 29 August with my two Erikas... I would definitely not have recognised my daughter if she had come on her own. She goes eagerly to school, in the family tradition in the *Melanchthongymnasium*...

Having spent some time in Wittenberg on his return, Hans settled as a solicitor in Berlin. But the end of the war was more troubling for his daughter Erika, as we shall see later.

Kate as refugee

A S WE HAVE SEEN, Kate Bosse and Dorothea, or Dolly, her sister, were the only girls allowed to attend Wittenberg's boys' grammar school, thanks to their father's influence. Kate then went to Munich University, to study classics, and chose Egyptology as part of her studies.[15] Taking advantage of the possibility of following courses at several German universities, Kate studied in Berlin and Bonn before graduating. The thesis of her doctorate, 'Human Figures in the Sculpture of the Late Egyptian Period', was published in Glückstadt in 1936, and republished in 1978.

Kate was supported by her parents, and spent some time in Italy,[16] Greece and Egypt, studying at museums in Berlin, Bologna, Florence and Turin. She also studied classical Arabic, Greek art and the history of the ancient world.

At the time Kate was courting Niklaus von Mossolow (variously referred to as Niki, Niky and Nika) who was a student in Munich, and he helped her with many drawings for her work. After Günther, Kate's brother, came to the university, the three went on a trip to Zugspitze, Germany's highest mountain.

Niki was the son of a Russian general, but his studies did not meet with much success. Some family letters note that he depended too much on Kate while working on his degree. They became engaged. But Paul Bosse was not thrilled, as he believed that Niki would not be successful in his profession. Later on he ordered both to break off their engagement, and it is likely that this happened, although it was not an easy thing for them to do.

The relationship influenced Kate – and her interest in Marxism was strengthened. She also started learning Russian and Italian. Together they went on tours to Russia and Italy and, at one stage, Kate researched in the Hermitage Museum in St Petersburg (Leningrad at that time).

Kate had been working in the Egyptology department of the German State Museum in Berlin since 3 September 1935 but, at the beginning of 1936, a colleague of hers, Alfred Hermann, drew the head of department's attention to the fact that she was of Jewish extraction. Although Rudolf Anthes, the head of department, did not want to release her, he had no choice but to fall in with Nazi laws prohibiting the employment of Jews in public posts. Kate was dismissed on 9 May 1936 and received a testimonial from Anthes on 11 May which noted 'as the prerequisite for Aryan origin had not been met, she cannot work any longer as an officer in the museum. I'm sorry to lose a capable colleague.' It was now clear that Kate could not work in Germany, and she had to start thinking about finding work abroad.

By the middle of September 1936, Kaethe Bosse, her mother, had already been in correspondence with Sir D'Arcy Thompson, who was a zoologist and classicist, in St Andrews, Scotland, in an attempt to find work for her daughter. It appears that a considerable effort had been made to find work for Kate, but that giving accommodation to a secretary had not been one of Sir D'Arcy's plans. He said in a letter to Kaethe Bosse:

> It is still true, of course, that none of my daughters wishes, or is able, to go to Germany at present, and that my wife and I had no idea of inviting a young Germany lady to live with us.
>
> But what you tell me of your daughter interests me very much, and I should much like to know more of her. I am now an old man, but have still much work to do. I have no secretary or typist, and have been thinking lately that I must have some such assistance next year; and if I do have an assistant it must be one who knows Greek, above all things!
>
> I am sending Fräulein Dr Käthe one or two small and unimportant papers – just enough to show her the kind of work I do. She must write me a letter about herself and her own work – and it would be nice and kind if she would send me a photograph of herself.[17]

As a result, when Kate came to Britain, it was as secretary to Sir D'Arcy Thompson firstly, and also later to Professor H. J. Roes, who was also a classicist.

Sir D'Arcy Thompson (1860–1948) was a renowned academic, a biologist and a mathematician, in addition to his work as a

classical scholar. His father, also named D'Arcy Thompson (1829–1902), had been professor of Greek at Queen's College, Galway. After graduating from Cambridge University, he was appointed professor at Dundee University in 1884, and then became professor of natural history in St Andrews University in 1917. His main work was *On Growth and Form* (1917) and he also took interest in the biological work of Aristotle.

Sir D'Arcy Thompson

Kate mentions the passage to England in her diary, at 10.15 on 15 January 1937:

> On the steamer *Bury* near the English coast. 'Fog.' We have been standing here in the same place since 11.30 last night. I suppose that I should already be sitting in the train to Liverpool. Tante Annie will be waiting; there are only travellers on the goods steamer...

Kate describes some of the other travellers in her diary, one man around 50 years old, with two missing fingers on his left hand. She talked to him about politics.

By 17 January, she had been to a church with Tante Annie. It's possible that Tante Annie was one of Kaethe Bosse's friends: she had spent some time in England when she was younger, in order to become fluent in English. The sermon was about a 'crooked man' and a 'crooked house' and a 'crooked mouse'. 'He describes these so warmly that we are all fonder of the "crooked house" than of the straight man on the narrow path,' is Kate's pithy remark.

On 2 March, she writes her diary in English, and it's clear that she is trying to master the language,

> Now, after six weeks, I could fairly write a book[18] filled with all the little charming stories of a nice university town, being a little bit beside the ordinary world of trouble, unrest and anxiety of war.
>
> There is the academic university: wives of professors, students, lecturers, there are the tea-parties, where people usually invite each other or following their social duty, or to make acquaintances.
>
> Here are the German people, united in this little place by the most different fates. There's the professor himself with his strange but charming peculiarities. There are strange Scotch Houses and ruins, in which a lot of well brought up ghosts still are living together with an anxious but faithful humanity. There is the nature, the sea, the rocks, the sea-gulls, sea birds, shells...

The cold weather begins to bite by 8 March: 'In a place like St Andrews the only way to keep warm is perpetual motion, mental and physical. You must walk… all day and then stand at a windswept street corner and argue about sin.' Staying in St Andrews wasn't likely to be the end of her journey. I vaguely remember that she once told me that she didn't have all that much work to do from Sir D'Arcy Thompson, and she looked for work farther afield, and had a promise of work in a school in Brighton.

By 23 March she mentions (this time in German) moving to London.

> In a week I shall be in London. A country of fables lies behind me. But I have put on weight and am becoming more tranquil, I have learnt a lot, I have learnt what it is to be a Scotsman and an Englishman, and have achieved some distance from the disruption at home. People here cannot understand Germany, more or less just as we cannot understand Russia. Every house is a castle, every person a castle. In London people are more 'continental', said Mrs Milne, the American.

Kate moved to take up residence in Tamar Lodge, 101 St George's Square, London, one of the grand streets of Pimlico. Here the Warwick Club provided her with accommodation at 35 shillings a week, inclusive of meals. Kate described her new situation,

> I spent my first weeks in London in the Warwick Club, where I could cook little things for myself on the gas oven. Breakfast and supper or lunch were mandatory – so that a person as a permanent guest could not make his own conditions. But with nothing more than a small room, one would pay 35 shillings for the flat and food. During the evening after supper the old women and the men who were more or less invalids would sit around the fire in the room, socialising: knitting, reading papers, talking now and again about parts of the empire where they had spent most of their lives, Africa or New Guinea or India.

In the middle of March she received a letter from F. Parkin, British & Continental Educational Agent, asking her to make an application for the post of an au pair to a teacher of students, giving German lessons and offering German conversation at Westcombe School, Dyke Road Avenue, Hove, Brighton. This was a private school for girls which could cater for around 80 pupils, but which was nearing the end of its life. Kate did not at first receive permission from the Home Office to become an au pair to Mrs Salmon at this school, but the Home Office asked her to present another application so that they could consider whether she could stay in the country. Kate was at the school for three months starting on 3 May. At the time she wrote:

> ... A special value was put on the school uniform... the better the school, the higher are the demands on a school uniform. Our little private school had 25 'boarders' and around 25 'day girls', with girls between the ages of seven and fifteen who wore the school uniform during the day and light summer attire during the evening. The uniform consisted of a tunic, a blouse with long arms, a jacket with the school coat of arms and the motto: *per aspera ad astra*, that most of the girls couldn't understand... The women teachers had to wear a hat and gloves in the street, in order not to harm the school's reputation.

Tamar Lodge, 101 St George's Square, London

Westcombe School, Duke Road Avenue, Brighton

The lessons included Latin and German, and Greek dancing, also elocution and sports, as well as the usual subjects. Kate's notes on her period in the school suggest that she was not in her element and that the girls there did not appreciate the opportunity to learn German.

During this period Kate exchanged letters with Niki, her betrothed. In a letter on 10 April, she thanks him for his letter but suggests that her own future is uncertain.

> A teaching post with pocket money of five shillings a week is not paradise, and the path towards obtaining a scholarship is very stony.

By 10 May, her letter to Niki suggests the difficulty of continuing a relationship from a distance.

> Nikuschka, you ask me whether I still keep a diary like the little green book. You do not understand one thing: at that time I was waiting, and every ounce of my energy changed into thoughts about you. Now you are active and all my energy is used.
>
> At that time I thought that I would win you, but the hope that remains is dim and weak and my path does no longer lead directly to you...

Efforts were afoot to arrange for Kate to go to America. H. Frankfort from the Oriental Institute in the University of Chicago had written on her behalf to several institutions, including the Metropolitan Museum of Art in New York, praising Kate's archaeological work and enquiring regarding the possibilities of a post. On 12 May a letter from H. E. Winlock, director of the Metropolitan Museum of Art, states: 'I see no prospect of enlarging the Egyptian department staff at present. I shall try to keep your letter in mind, however, and if anything occurs to me, I would be very glad to let you know.'

Dr Gurney from Bristol had already looked for support from America on Kate's behalf. He had corresponded with academics at Princeton University, New Jersey, and had suggested that

Kate could get in touch with Professor E. Erzfeld, the Iranian scholar, who had been in Berlin. President Park at Bryn Mawr, Pennsylvania, was another possibility, as was Professor E. A. Lowe who was at the time at Balliol College, Oxford.

A letter from Toledo, Ohio, on 8 June 1937, states:

> There is no chance in Toledo for Dr Bosse. I had occasion recently to appeal to the Toledo Museum of Art for someone else for whom they were unable to make a place... Conceivably a place might be found for Dr Bosse at Bryn Mawr College in Bryn Mawr, Pennsylvania, near Philadelphia.

In spite of this, on 24 June, a letter from H. Frankfort offered a possibility of work:

> There is a possibility of a combined Museum-University job, which presumably would mean teaching hieroglyphs and arranging the collections.
>
> Professor Speiser, who teaches Assyriology there [Philadelphia] writes [to] me that he considers the chances for an appointment for one or two years to be better than 50 per cent. A permanent appointment could of course not be expected until you have shown your worth.

Kate did not go to America, and one must presume that nothing came of these offers.

But she had not put the past completely behind her. In one note she says that everything that she wore reminded her of 'Nika' (Niky):

> My scarf... the reddish brown of my clothes... my wristwatch, the steel band, which we obtained together, the coat... and yet... Everything I do is under Nika's influence... At the moment, as I see that I can support myself, I have had an answer to one question. I shall live this year as if it were a preparation for Nika. I'm aware that I have a chance once again. After this year I shall be ready...

At the time Kate was living in the home of Mrs Gurney, 2 Brunswick Mansion, Handel Street, London WC1. Her mother wrote her a card to say that she had sent her two letters, and that Niky had gone with Hans and Günther's wife to Meissen. She also added that Paul was glad to have received a letter from Kate.

Kate then became secretary to Dr A. S. Yahuda, who was a Hebrew and Arabic scholar, and then she was given a position with Professor Stephen Glanville at University College, London. He was head of the Egyptology department, and Kate was given some lecturing work and an opportunity to do some research at the Petrie Museum. The Society for the Protection of Science and Learning arranged this, and the wife of Sir Clough Williams-Ellis of Portmeirion was one of the members of this body. 'Penrhyndeudraeth' (the village on the north-western Welsh coast near the Portmeirion estate created by Sir Clough) was the first Welsh word that Kate used, as she wrote a card of thanks to this Society. She received support also from Professor Dr Alexander Scharff, the Egyptology professor of Munich University, in her application for a research post, as she had been a student of his for several semesters there.

On 27 July 1938, with reference to Kate, when she applied for a permanent position, Professor Glanville said this of her:

> Dr Bosse came here a year ago with a six months' grant... to carry on with her research work... and this grant was renewed on my recommendation last January.
>
> She is a very diligent worker with a sound knowledge of Egyptian archaeology and sufficient linguistic competence to use inscriptional material for her purpose. Her training in classical archaeology is of great value for the work she is now engaged on, Egyptian iconography...
>
> In addition to her research work she has been of great assistance to me in the museum attached to this department in classifying and registering objects as well as re-arranging their exhibition for

teaching purposes. Finally I have on several occasions been able to ask her to take seminar classes for me in my absence, and this she has done efficiently and with enthusiasm... it is with great regret that we have to face the prospect of losing her owing to the inevitable termination of her grant.

During this period it was possible for Kate to correspond with the family in Germany. She succeeded in keeping in touch with the family until the start of the war. In one letter her mother describes a journey through Holland. She also mentions travelling to England, when she and Paul visited Kate.

12 September 1937

My dearest Katrinchen,

We are now happily back at home, and when we arrived yesterday, Niki and the others were in the station. He is working diligently for his doctorate, and he is coming here in October to work for 10 days.

The whole journey was a perfect dream. On the way back, the big industrialist, who continually received invitations to England, and who had thus not used his money, lent us the money for the lovely car journey through Holland – and Holland is really wonderful in respect of its tidiness and the wealth of its people, the charming houses into which one can see far inside, no-one has anything to hide, so that I also find Leyden to be a very beautiful place. In any case, my love, we had such a view of the expanses, in a way that I had never dreamt...

I'm ever more appreciative of the benefit we had from the journey to England, in every way – Opa [Paul] does not need to take his sleeping medicine any more, that hasn't happened for years. Today there are practices for air raids. Nicky has fetched papers for the purpose – it is a little bit strange in the darkness here. At least it's quite easy to do this in our attic room. It's possible to darken things here easily. But it's not so easy at work in the clinic. Fritz is now ready and I'm quite glad that he's studying... Opa has a lot of patients from quite far-off places,

many more than in the hospital... Someone asked Opa if he was
now going to the hospital, and Opa answered, 'I only go to clinics
now, not to small hospitals.'

Kate describes this visit in a letter to Tante Annie (around 16
September 1937):

I don't want you to wait too long a time for my letter about Vati
and Mutti's visit, though it is already more than a week that they
went home. Time passes so quickly in London.

We had a splendid time together, they lived quite near to
my room and all the days we had a surprisingly good weather,
Italianlike blue sky and beautifully warm sunshine.

They arrived only about midnight on Thursday the 2. IX
(as you know, they came together with a kind of *Reisegesellschaft*
[travel agent]) but having had a beautifully quiet crossing they were
very fresh.

We went with the Reisegesellschaft only to see Windsor and
Eton on Sunday, all the other time we spent together seeing
London life, streets, parks, traffic, Vati was especially pleased by
the big escalators of the London underground stations and Mutti
by the beautiful shops with English good material and good
food, which, so it seems, they are missing more and more in
Germany. But they and all the other Germans were mostly pleased
by the freedom of speech and not having to be afraid of spies. I
imagine that it is worse than any other difficulty of life in modern
Germany.

I had lunch and dinner together with them in their hotel, as
Vati wanted badly to pay something for me, though I had got a
birthday present of £10 from Professor Newberry, who knew that
Vati and Mutti were going to stay with me.

At home everything seems to be alright. The clinic is growing
very quickly and all their food they get from Fritz's farm. Two
days ago I got a letter from Mutti, telling me that they arrived
safely at home after having had a very nice trip in car throughout
Holland. I am so glad that they had the short holiday after so many
years of hard work.

In October 1937 her mother urges her not to give up on her Egyptological studies, and she has also arranged for her to visit Germany over Christmas:

> But I want one thing, my love, I don't want you to cut down every Egyptological bridge behind you, I've just heard from Niky that the man who has a non-Aryan wife, who is writing something similar, has had a position in Switzerland. I was thinking that one should keep one's eyes open, and that one someday you could use the knowledge that was won so diligently.
>
> With Niky one thing is clear! Without you he will never finish. Without you he won't embark on a new study and won't be able to do that... Dolly believes that there is a new law today, if someone marries a foreigner, one can still be a German. That would be very reasonable. So are matters, dear Katrinchen...
>
> Mainly because of your journey over Christmas I went to Berlin. That was also good. Because of the post I had a completely senseless answer from the travel agency. So it is only possible to do this if one uses a German steamer. Otherwise the prospects for exchanging money are uncertain. Therefore you would have to pay for the journey from Southampton and back yourself. The journey costs around 6.50M. I'm sending 15 Schillings to you today. The steamer belongs to Norddeutschen Lloyd, Hamburg, and leaves Southampton on 16.12 and arrives at Hamburg on December the 17th. Now Vati says that I'm writing pure drivel. You can thus come with the Hansa on 22 December and travel back with the Hansa again on 6 January. Write immediately to say if this is alright. I'll order the tickets at once.

During this period, as has been seen, the family's minds turn to the possibilities of emigrating, either to North or South America, where some members of the family were living already. After relating the death of her sister, Kaethe offers some possibilities to arrange a way for Hans, her brother, and for the rest of them, to emigrate:

8 December '37

My dear daughter,

…

Enclosed then is a note:

Otto Ludwig, Philadelphia, gives the affidavit. The addresses are in the note. Karl Hentschel, Mexico, a friend from his younger days whom Opa had supported, has sent an invitation by telegraph to go to America.

An uncle of Erika's father lives in Cleveland, Ohio. He has already celebrated his golden wedding. That is why Erika isn't sure whether he is still alive. Wilhelm Sporke is his name. His daughter, Frau Martesen, lives there as well and the addresses are in the note.

I'm sending you a picture of Young Ingrid. Then our cousin, Ulrich Ledien, a doctor, lives in Chicago, Surfstreet 638… after all, he is also a relative. I believe that is enough.

My dearest, how lovely is it that you can write about coffee and pancakes in Oxford Street. I think then about our two lovely trips this year and last year. All that seems an age ago.

The Tippens have had their St Nicholas.[19] How sweet and peaceful it is when Tippen recites a story so intelligently with his little voice… And then Tante Eva, who is now in heaven. I hope now that the dear Lord has had his quota with one woman…

… have you any requests for books? Because books, as far as I know, are still tax-free. Write soon if you can.

A kiss from my heart,

OMA

During the year Kate is torn between a wish to stay in England and returning to Germany. By now conditions at home in Germany were not easy, as is testified by her diary:

Friday, 14.1.1938

I'm trying to set myself a new aim. What do I wish, what can I wish?

At home? It is not a home for me. No room belongs to me. If I am out for a while, Vati cannot sleep for hours. If Niki wants a bath, there would be so many difficulties. If I helped him with the work, they would accuse me of looking tired.

Get married in Germany. Imagine a marriage with Onkel Gugu. If only he could be a doctor. But me a dutiful wife in today's Germany – ! In England the picture is different, but there are so many miserable traditions here.

Everything insists: be independent. In Germany I've 'become extinct'.

So over the expanse of water.

Perhaps even to Africa.

If Niki was not one of those passionate Mongols –

By now I have to teach myself to see that I've become an unnatural burden for him. But I feel sad that I couldn't help with the last 5 pages. I would have liked to have brought my task to an end.

In the meantime, it is clear that Kate still harbours strong feelings for Niki, but their relationship is now impossible. Her brother, Günther, known in his family by the pet name 'Onkel Gugu', was now married, and this makes Kate contemplate her own position.

31 March 1938

This afternoon I went to Regents Park in the lovely fresh spring sunshine, a sea breeze, blue skies, the green chestnut trees, green lawns one can sit on, and the din of the city hardly to be heard. I don't know if Onkel Gugu has noticed in some letters that I have, during the last few weeks, fought the bravest battle against the greatest of all gods, who forces me in every way to love an Englishman, fie the devil. And in this clear sunshine, I could also ask more questions one after the other. What do you really want? Have you come so far that life is peaceful, a caring 'husband', who, when it is possible, cooks for you, and who, so politely, can satisfy you – But there is still the devilish feeling that one has become so distanced from the 'dreams of youth'. Forgive my frequent cursing… But I still have the dream that I want to be a PARTNER to a PRODUCTIVE person, NOT A PASSIVE

ONE; that I continue with my life's work, if I forget that. But I'm afraid of the day when I'll tell myself: live in the most comfortable way, everything is so unimportant *sub specie aeternitatis*;[20] or worse, if I persuade myself that an angelic English marriage of that type is the only right thing for me, exactly what Oma wishes for me.

With her brother married, what is interesting is that Kate rebels against being contented in a conventional relationship.

In her diary during that year, Kate expresses concern regarding the future, and her dilemma is obvious. She questions herself, and there are some English phrases in her German notes:

4.4.1938

What do you want?
   Have roots.
Where would you like to be?
   In Germany.
Why don't you return?
   Because I'm not allowed to be in Germany during war.
   Because I have more chains in Germany than as a worker here.
You won't go under any condition?
   There is one condition – but it is a part of the ballast that has already been thrown out.
What remains for you therefore: *face reality*.
   1) *woman courier*
   2) *secretary*
   3) marry a man with whom you can have children.
You still have time for number 3. You're afraid to lose your ideal. But you will still come across the 'Father for your children'. So there is no reason to be perturbed. Always do what is around you.
   Don't load the ship too heavily!
   Vati and Mutti will be disappointed!
   For God's sake, be independent…
   Only you can live your own life!

In the meantime, in the keeping with her left-wing views, Kate joined the Bloomsbury Left Book Club, and had a stormy relationship with a man called Stanley, who came from Sheffield and who had studied French and Spanish at Oxford. He had arranged summer schools for the Left Book Club, and earned some sort of a living by marking examination papers. It is clear from the letters that they had a close relationship, including enjoyment of music, walks and what lovers do. Stanley had graduated in 1932. To Kate he represented the loyal Englishman, having been obedient to church, king and country as a boy scout. He was more of a communist than socialist, and among his interests were playing the violin and chess.

On 10 November, Kate writes to Stanley, and according to the mood of the letter it appears that the relationship is fading, and there is also discomfort regarding his relationship with other lovers:

> It is half past ten. I am sitting in my room, the washed underwear on the horse in front of the fire before me and your broken but burning lamp standing on the chimney piece, while the melodies of Beethoven's 'C Major Quartet' which I played on the gramophone just now, still resounding in my mind.
>
> It is a strange thing about 'being proud', 'sense of honour' and all the other sentiments which grow like weeds on the ground of uncertain affection. So, all I can do is to let things go for a moment, to retire into 'splendid isolation' and to try to think.
>
> Dear me, what are we doing. We follow our instincts like barbarians. Instincts which are tyrannised by scores of conscious and unconscious prejudices.
>
> And what could we do! Instead of fighting like schoolboys against each other. How could we 'exchange' the traditions of our nations, how could we enjoy these fine and noble pleasures of music, nature, poetry, sport, handcrafts – yes I say so and I mean it – and relax from the mania which surrounds us. We ought to remember and we must learn, even in the 12th hour, that love-making is an art not only of the body but of the minds. That rules want to be created and observed – don't change partners so easily and quickly. Would you do that in rowing?

On 12 January 1939, Kaethe's letter to her daughter again displays how many members of the family are thinking of emigrating, giving up their stable life. She mentions the possibility that Kate should go to Sweden or America:

> Günther and Knubben [his wife] came back from Sweden. They wanted you to tell them what form you want the advert for Sweden to be. It's definitely wise to have many irons in the fire. But I believe time after time that England is the country of your choice...
>
> We have all appreciated very much your efforts on behalf of Hans. I'll give him the woman's address. Liesbeth Stürmer mentioned a family going to Peru, but said that the climate there is quite unhealthy. I hope that he [Hans] will have an affidavit soon. Have you applied for the states of mid America, which you mention in the context of a year's citizenship?
>
> Knubben's mother wants to write to the aunt in question, in America, on your behalf. Even if you don't need this, it won't harm anyone, Günther will send you the pictures. Let us know immediately if we can send you *Wurst* and which books I should send you...

The family had been sending some money to Kate in England, but circumstances made it impossible for this to continue. Hans was hoping to go to South America, and Dolly was facing difficulties with her work as a doctor following pressure on Germans not to visit her surgery. In the midst of their own troubles, Kate's parents were glad that she had started her own life in Britain in spite of the possibilities of emigrating further afield. Her mother's letter on 17 January 1939 suggests this:

> Dear Kathe,
>
> Your dear letter today was a real treat for me and Vati, and we were happy all day after receiving it. I'm sending you the Inselbücher [books by the Insel publisher] which you wanted to have. There are 16 books by Insel and two others. Should I

send you a catalogue? I'm glad that you are getting your things in order, so it's a pleasure to send you something new.

It's so lovely that you're feeling so well over there. That makes Vati and me so happy. So you know that it's no longer possible to send you the 20 Marks? Have you had money since November?

Hans is going tomorrow to Berlin, in order to find out how things are getting on with Montevideo or Domaigo (I believe that is the name). He hasn't had news from Mexico, but that of course will take some time, and Hans is a little impatient. You know that he is now getting used to just spiritual work and naturally he's suffering greatly from doing nothing, especially as he cannot drive a car.

People have a lot of sympathy for him, as he is such an honourable man.

Yesterday and the day before Tippen[21] was here. He's doing his very best to come back again to the house and he calls on Opa to ask if he can stay here.

I've had your pictures of Egypt framed in lovely old silver frames for Vati. He's got a lot of work, the weather here is miserable, and many people are ill. It's good that Günther, who has had an excellent training, helps him. You know that medical studies here have been curtailed by almost two years, and Fritz by a year. The year of practical medical work will be put into the study year.

Heken[22] was here yesterday, it's always so happy here when she is around, and she does the work of two. Paula's business has not been decided yet. She must (i.e. her mother) go immediately once again to the health officer. Well I hope that will succeed. I hope that for the poor girl.

Dolly seems a little worried. I wish she could find someone eventually who could take her. She is just as Vati was previously and so it is with every doctor. I hope she will get better soon. She is like most doctors in believing the worst all the time. Write something to her to lift her heart.

A host of warm greetings and a loving kiss,
Mutti

Kate received a letter from Somerville College, Oxford on 25 January 1939 offering her a research grant, with work at the Ashmolean Museum, where an Egyptological collection had just opened. A letter from Helen Darbishire said 'you have been very warmly recommended to us' and that they had a 'grant for research to a scholar who is in this country as a refugee'.

At Somerville College, as a senior member, with her own room and a seat on the High Table, she met J. Gwyn Griffiths. He was a Baptist minister's son, from Pentre, Rhondda. An ardent Welsh-speaker, he was an early member of Y Blaid Genedlaethol – the Welsh National Party – that was established in 1925 with the aim of safeguarding the Welsh language and securing self-government for Wales. She was introduced to him by Abd el-Mohsen Bakir, or 'Wncwl Mochsen' to us when we were children. Gwyn wondered whether the two were in a relationship, but that did not prevent him kindling a friendship with Kate. Gwyn at the time was a research student at Queen's College and he would spend much of his time in the Griffith Egyptological Institute in the Ashmolean building.[23]

Stanley was still around in the background, although he was married to a girl called Karen. He said, in a note dated 12 March 1939, 'I'll unbosom myself to you later in the week. I am thinking of coming up to Oxford next weekend with Karen – would you like to meet her? Or are the greenstick fractures our hearts sustained too recently mended? I leave it to you sister.'

By 18 May 1939, it seems that Stanley had left his wife. He writes to Kate asking her to meet him 'outside Woolworth's at 6.15', saying he's looking forward to seeing her again, and adds this about his wife: 'A much more amusing, and as little founded, beldame story, is that she is going round telling the world that I have taken to drink since I left her!'

Arrangements were made during the summer of 1939 for

Kate to go to Holland to meet her father, and Kaethe wrote to her daughter to suggest the arrangements:

29 June '39

... it seems to me that Scheveningen is the correct choice. Opa will write to you how far the money will extend and how long he can wait. I believe that Lushey has already shown you how well off you are there. It must be wonderful there. It appears to us that all the lovely things you're experiencing are wonderful. If I can get you something nice to read to your friends, do write.

With the difficulties in Germany increasing, and the relationship with Stanley at an end, the position in the Ashmolean gave Kate some stability. Scarcely would she have thought that this position, indirectly, would draw her for ever away from England.

Love in the
shadow of war

L OVE BLOSSOMING BETWEEN THE bookshelves of the Ashmolean? Kate was looking for a husband who could father her children. But she also wanted an exciting marriage, in which she could keep her independent spirit and be creative. Although Germany was still drawing her back in her mind, returning was not possible. But her future in Britain was still in doubt, and the shadow of war hung over the country, with her family in Germany having to experience increasing constraints and crises.

Gwyn had returned to study at Oxford during March 1937, having spent five months as an archaeological assistant digging in Sesebi, Wadi Halfa, Sudan, under a scheme run by the Egypt Exploration Society. His college career had followed the same subjects as Kate's, the Classics and Egyptology. He had graduated in 1933 with a first-class honours degree in Greek from the University College of Wales, Cardiff, and then spent a year on a teacher's training course. He later worked on an M.A. thesis on the influence of Ancient Egypt on Greek and Mycenaean religious cults before the Hellenistic Age at Liverpool University. Having returned from Sudan, and having become a fellow of the University of Wales, he started as a senior student at Queen's College, Oxford, studying for a Ph.D. on the quarrel between Horus and Seth.

The two met early in 1939 when Kate was working in the Ashmolean and living at Somerville College. Is seems that their

J. Gwyn Griffiths

relationship developed fervently, and by July she had met one of Gwyn's brothers and also his friend Pennar Davies, who was to become a highly-respected literary and religious figure in Wales. When Gwyn then spent some time studying at the British Museum in London, a passionate correspondence ensued.

Both wrote to each other at least every four days during the July of that year. War casts a dark shadow over the letters, and these discuss attitudes in Germany and Wales towards the pending conflict. The first letter from Kate to Gwyn is on 3 July 1939. She mentions someone she had encountered who had left the Sudetenland after Hitler's invasion, fleeing to a camp for refugees in Czechoslovakia. He then left the camp in Prague on the same day as Hitler's arrival, and narrowly avoided being taken to a concentration camp with the remainder of the refugees. He lived beyond the law in Prague, and managed to cross the border to Poland and went to the British Embassy there. Kate says in her letter:

> He also told us about the unnecessary cruelties which happened during the occupation, things which I dislike to repeat, as, after all, they concern my own countrymen and I felt ashamed in a double sense; ashamed because German people could change so quickly and ashamed that we all of us here are inclined to forget about the unjust sufferings which are going on and on, just because we are safe at the moment.
>
> A more amusing incident was that some newly converted Nazis who had to confiscate forbidden books had been rather too keen and in the case of this refugee (as in many others) Goethe and Schiller had the honour to be burnt together with Marx and Lenin.

Literature and Egyptology are frequent themes in their correspondence, reflecting their mutual interests. The letter ends by mentioning poems which they had exchanged, and then there are notes on Egyptological minutiae.

In his reply on 6 July, from 31 Rosedene Gardens, Ilford, Essex,[24] Gwyn starts with a grammatical explanation:

Fy[1] anwylaf[2] *Käthe*

At the bottom of the page is an explanatory footnote:

(1) Possessive pronoun, 1st person sing.
(2) Superlative degree of adjective 'annwyl', 'liebe'.

Gwyn had already sent her an English sonnet he'd composed about the dawn. He then continues with personal information:

> It was an event to have your first letter, and I have read it many times. (Who was the Londoner who wished to correct your English?) I was struck by its muscled sobriety of style, and by the indefatigable patience to which the handwriting clearly points. Knowing you as I do, I tend to disbelieve all theories about handwriting and personality.

You ought to be interested in my career, so I should tell you that I have not been appointed at Swansea University, but have an interview for Nottingham University next Friday (Classics and Ancient History). The latter is not such a good post but would be better than a school. Professor Tillyard of Cardiff advises me to try for a Commonwealth Fellowship to America during the winter, if I fail to find a university.

My work: Monday, Tuesday, Wednesday have yielded each two pages only. They are foolscap pages, and contain difficult material. I hope to write more, however, today...

> I miss you very much.
>
> Love,
>
> Gwyn

Kate writes another letter on 7 July 1939:

Mein liebster Gwyn,

...

Thank you for your note with your sonnet that gives words to the contrast in our lives: dwelling on antique thoughts and ideals and kept awake by the machines of the industrial age...

Kate shows an interest in Wales and Rhondda, and says in a letter on 11 July 1939:

You know, when one's mind is specially occupied with a name or person one is bound to find it suddenly everywhere. In the same way I go on hearing and reading about Wales and Welshmen and Swansea and Cardiff. I cut out a few newspaper notes that might interest you. Have you seen 'Rhondda Roundabout'?[25]

The remainder of the letter discusses books on Egyptology, and at the top of the letter, Kate, realising this, says in English and then in German: 'I wanted to tell you *how sweet and full of longing is the smell of lime flowers in the College garden* – but there you are – the whole letter about books!'

The first two pages of Gwyn's response on 13 July deals

entirely with linguistic matters before he then relates the attitudes of the poor people of Sudan:

> Actually, they have quite a considerable past to glory in... And there is no danger that the English will teach them any nationalism which will involve political liberty. When I was in the Sudan (which, incidentally, has the reputation of being the best-governed province in the Empire), it made me almost sick to find little dark children kissing my hands, as though I were a demi-god. How I longed for a little self-respect and independence!
>
> You are quite right, of course, in deprecating the feverishness of modern nationalism in almost all its forms. It is very easy to do so, however, behind the guise of Imperialism. I would remind you of your Communist sympathies.

Not having known each other for more than a few months, it is surprising that they are already talking about marriage. Gwyn states,

> We shall have time to discuss these and many other matters when you come here in August. I confess I am looking forward with zest to seeing you in a new role – as Hausfrau, and as mine. The prospect is indeed happy, and we must soon be fixing dates.

Gwyn was not appointed at Nottingham. In a letter on 17 July Kate makes arrangements to meet Gwyn at the British Museum, but says that she wants to spend some of her holidays in August with her family, before ending, 'I have some fears for my "Hausfrauenrolle" [role as housewife] but I hope we shall find some way to realize our plans.'

On 21 July, after exchanging further letters, Kate replies,

> *Mein liebster* Gwyn,
>
> ...
>
> Tonight after dinner we had a quite interesting talk in the S.C.R. about the state of mind of German University professors just before Hitler and the 3rd Reich. Frau B. attacked them so eagerly that I became almost Fascist in order to keep a little self-respect for

my country: how they had been one sided specialists not caring about the education of their pupils, envious of the fame of their colleagues etc.

Miss Sutherland told an amusing story, how in the beginning of 1933 they had arranged a conference of German and English teachers, in order to interchange democratic ideas, and how, as Hitler had just taken power, there came not the people they had invited but newly converted and very eager Nazis in their place...
Write soon.
Es küsst Dich
Deine Käthe
In the *Spectator* of 14 July I found a letter of Dafydd Jenkins about 'The Welsh Language'. Have you seen it?

Gwyn replies on 22 July:

Fy Anwylaf Käthe, [Dearest Kate]

...

I had not myself forgotten your stela[26] on Thursday night. But our time was short. And with all due respects to our common academic interests, you are more important than the stela, and all other stelae put together. It is strange what an urgency I have felt about you this week; as though the winds of love were blowing to tempest strength. And yet, when I recall your charms, your beguiling ways, your shining loveliness, it isn't strange at all! It would be thrilling to know that you are my Escape-Me-Never...

Mutually appreciative letters follow, and on 24 July Kate talks of her own nature:

So many thanks for your dear letters which give me more and more the confidence that you are really able to give me that support and that affection which I need so much. You wrote about that spot of pity which you recognize in your love. To be quite frank: As much as I dislike pity (you are very clever in recognising Nietzsche as my teacher) I think I almost encouraged you to pity me by telling about the nunnery, by showing you the poem about 'Einsamkeit' [loneliness]. I showed you where I am vulnerable as

I know (and as you prove more and more) that you have gifts of *Geist und Herz* [spirit and heart] which only want to be discovered in order to develop freely. I wonder whether you know your own value.

She then says that she had spent a day with Mochsen, the academic Egyptian who was a personal friend of Gwyn at Oxford.

Kate's letters arrive before she prepares for the journey to go to Holland to see her father, without knowing that this would be the last time for them to see one another. Gwyn writes with appreciation:

I have heard your voice, by now, in Rilke. Yes the authentic tones:

'*Es ist gut, einsam zu sein, denn Einsamkeit ist schwer; dass etwas schwer ist, muss uns ein Grund mehr sein, es zu tun!*'

[It is good to be lonely, as loneliness is difficult; that something is difficult is of necessity a reason for us to do it!']

This is your theory about *Schwierigkeiten* [difficulties] alright. But it doesn't agree, in this particular matter, with your poem '*Einsamkeit*'.

As for my loneliness, I assure you it is mostly of your making. Although my recent solitude has been more than I have generally known – after all, to be quite alone in a house isn't very pleasant – yet its intense quality is entirely due to you.

On second thoughts, you may bring the typewriter, unless it's too much trouble… Of course, you can leave it with me when you go to Holland.

By 3 August, Gwyn looks forward to having Kate call on him on her way to Holland.

… Now when I say '*Wie ich liebe dich!*' how many mistakes are here? That is surely not a Subordinate Clause, but an important statement. I am all expectancy, my sweet. The house is not quite as ready as I am – you will have to forgive male incompetence…

I expect you will have plenty of suggestions how we shall spend

our time together. We shall find the time all too short, I am sure!
Still, there will be a chance for both of us to reveal all our qualities
so that nothing shall be hid.
Enjoying the present and planning the future…
Au revoir, meine Liebste!

Kate managed to spend some time with Gwyn, and
on 13 August she writes to Gwyn from the Grand Hotel,
Scheveningen,

Gwyn dear,

… In the afternoon we went to the aerodrome to meet my father,
brother and nephew who arrived almost an hour late via Leipzig-
Köln. At 7 we arrived in Scheveningen, which is comparatively
empty for August but the weather is promising…
Yesterday I remembered a conversation about the eternal
problem man-woman.
He: That is just the trouble that women are so 'unprincipled'
devils!
She: That is the trouble that men are so 'principled' devils.

The letter then continues in German:

I was sitting with my brother after supper in a little café, listening
to Viennese music; "You're a silly boy," I thought then, "You
want me to prove that I love you. Only with the intellect can
one prove. And as soon as I give you reasons, you say, That is so
contrived! You're like a child breaking a doll to pieces, in order to
see what's inside."

We both then sat together for a long time and [the letter now
turns to English] in addition to conversations about politics my
brother, Fritz, told me how he wanted to prepare his house first
before marrying though he had not looked for a bride yet, and was
sure to have many difficulties before being allowed to marry an
'Aryan'. It is strange and very refreshing experience to be together
with one's brother (by the way he is hardly taller than you), a male
mind but without the disturbances of sexual attraction, perhaps
the only real friendship possible between the two sexes, or should

a friendship of similar affection and value be possible after '*die Leidenschaft flieht, die Liebe muss bleiben*' [for passion will fly, but love must be surviving] as Schiller says in his poem '*die Glocke*' [the bell]. We even practise English together.

The stories I hear about Germany are depressing enough, especially the strain on their nerves by the constantly changing laws (the only thing constant left) is immense… If I went back I probably would be forced to work in munitions factories. You can believe me how little I am longing to do that and especially forced!

My father told me that he had bought new dining room furniture for me made out of light wood and in very good style. But he thinks that to take over furniture I would have to give up German citizenship… He also gave me some valuable things.

Kate in Scheveningen with her father and nephew, Tippen. This is the last time she saw her father

The Grand Hotel, Scheveningen, where Kate and her family stayed. It was demolished in 1974

Gwyn answers from Ilford on 15 August, and they finally agree to marry. War is now clearly on the horizon and Gwyn has strong convictions on the responsibility of the Christian:

I am having some fun with my democratic speech.[27] I find as my basic principle that dictatorship has throughout history been the result of war or revolution. Therefore the crux of my matter will be the importance of our attitude to war. Another war will indubitably mean the making fascist of the democratic countries – the thing is already happening – and it will mean further dictatorships and revolutions when it is over. The chief duty of the Christian Church is the duty which it willingly undertook in the first three centuries: to refuse to co-operate in war, and to generate the common desire that war must be avoided at all costs. You see that I am a trained rebel: that my thought is earnestly post-revolutionary in the Christian sense, if pre-revolutionary in the Communist sense.

Love is the last subject of the letter:

I was reading a piece from one of Shaw's prefaces last night. He was saying that most happy unions were formed on the basis of money, common interests, congeniality, and mundane affinity; and not love. In ten years' time I shall perhaps be wiser. But at the moment I am not thrilled at the suggestion. And though I know we have common interests (not much money, alas), congenialities etc etc etc: nothing matters to me now but that I love you, yes, in the primitive, pre-revolutionary, fleshly, bodily, sexual, all-inclusive way. Put that in your pipe and smoke it, you bewitching heart-snatcher!

A thousand-and-one kisses
Dein Gwyn

Kate's future in the United Kingdom is uncertain, and she says in a letter to Gwyn on 17 August 1939:

To tell the worst first. It is quite impossible for me to get away this week. I shall return on Thursday 24th as my visum expires on the 25th. I am really very sorry that I shall not be able to see you for

139

such a long time but you know how strong family ties can be and I am quite occupied with cheering up people.

That is the only reason too, for my going out almost every night to teach my brother the art of enjoying oneself which is quite forgotten in Nazi-Germany. To tell you one example. There was in W. [Wittenberg] a Fräulein von S., 20 years old who was not strong enough to do *Arbeitsdienst* [work service] but was allowed instead of that to do a year's work as *Kindergärtnerin* [nursery teacher]. My brother was a good friend with her and together with my sister-in-law and my other brother they had nice evening parties etc. Suddenly she was sent away from W. to another place because she had been a friend with my brother, *id est* people of partly Jewish extraction. My brother went to several '*Behörden*' [authorities] proving that if der Führer himself had been photographed together with my father, there was no reason to avoid our family. He even got people to agree that he was not the reason for Frl. v. S's '*Versetzung*' [transfer] – but the facts remained nevertheless…

But worse than everything is the inconsistency; every day new laws, partly opposite to earlier ones and everybody uses them as he likes or as far as he is not opposed by somebody of higher rank.

Your sermon seems to be logically alright and has only that against it, that Germany would not fight against Poland if she knew that England would fight. So the only thing to avoid war is to threaten war, a *circulus vitiosus* [vicious circle] or as it is said [she then writes in German] *that our sins have a home in our children until the third or fourth generation*. Still, I am willing to agree that it is good to have an Ethic which remains true to itself in spite of consequences.

This Ethic, of course, is bound to be wrong at certain points, as anything rigid, but to follow Nietzsche, a lie consistently obeyed is *Kulturbildend* [culture forming] otherwise there would be no art, no form, no society…

To come back to the business part. I am afraid I have to ask you to pack my belongings and take them to the Student Movement House. It is rather bad luck.

Kate is still in Holland on 19 August, but this time she has had the pleasure of being with some members of her family. Thoughts on feelings and love get attention in this letter:

> More than for a long time before I felt during the last weeks how much I need being loved. Yes, love from father, brother, child's love and your love, *mein Geliebter* [dearest]...
>
> I remember the saying of a doctor-poet, Schleich (in '*die Weisheit der Freude*' [the wisdom of joy]) *Ein Mann kann durch vieles glücklich werden – die Frau nur durch Liebe* [Man can be happy through many things – but only through love can a woman be happy].
>
> [She continues in German] And this love is nature – and connected to the body, like the love you write about in your letters, and this love insists and demands the union of body and soul.
>
> [She now changes to English] There is a slight possibility that I come before Thursday but only if the political situation turns to the worse.

By 20 August Gwyn is back in Rhondda, at his parents' home, Bryn Hyfryd, St Stephen's Avenue, Pentre. With him is Gwilym, his younger brother. Elizabeth (Bessie), his elder sister (who died with her husband, the Rev. Huw Jones, in an accident in the manse of Y Gopa, Pontarddulais, some years later) was in Ilfracombe, Augusta (Ogi), his other sister, was in Weston-super-Mare, Gwyn's parents were in west Wales, and David his brother was away preaching, but all were likely to come home the following weekend.

Kate returned shortly after this to Britain. War was imminent. She hoped in a letter on 24 August, that she would have some financial security through her family:

> The British Museum closed, probably to carry the most precious antiquities out of danger. Everywhere posters giving information about air-raid signals and in addition to that the shock of the Nazi-Soviet pact!! What a world, dear.

I do not want to keep secret from you that I see at least a possibility now to improve our financial calamities, of course only if there is no war. My father thinks that I can take a '*Hypothek*' [mortgage] in England on my house in Baden, or that failing that I could exchange it with a house in England and then sell that. I shall have to research into it... We calculated that, interests paid, there might be left £1,000. Only if!!

As there is nothing left in London to attract my sense of duty or of pleasure I shall fulfil myself a wish I have had for a long time, already before I knew you. I shall go to North Wales into the mountains to-morrow, if possible to Bettws-y-coed. I have an idea that with walking and studying the Welsh books I bought to-day I may manage to keep myself out of the 'war-psychosis' as long as possible. There is even a little hope left that you will come and see me before I go back to Oxford.

The decision to go to Betws-y-coed was sudden and unexpected. This was the first place in Wales that Kate visited, and she went there without giving Gwyn any notice of this. Kate finishes the letter after arriving at Betws-y-coed, and securing lodging at Church Hill, Heol Bryn Conwy.

Hurrah, here I am in the middle of the mountains and intending to stay here for at least a week, if! –
In the case 'if' would you mind ringing me up.
Write soon, good luck.
Your photo has got an honoured position on the mirror.
Love
Kate

When he received the letter from Kate postmarked Betws-y-coed, Gwyn wishes he was with her:

I am glad you have left the Metropolis. And with what magnificent swiftness you did it! You will soon be out-Hitlering Hitler himself. And to think that you are in the heart of the real 'mountains' in Betws-y-coed! I confess that nothing has ever moved me to such passionate longing as to think of Käthe in Betws-y-coed. The thought makes me wild. And your kind warm words increase my yearning ten-fold... You have set my blood in a whirlwind.

Alas, I'm afraid I cannot accept the most adorable invitation I have ever had. If war comes, I shall have to see you soon. If not – and things seem a little more hopeful today – my original plan was to return to London at the end of next week or a little later...

You may have wondered why I have not suggested your coming here to my home. Actually the idea is not immediately possible, owing to sheer lack of room. My sister is not returning yet to Ilford owing to the crisis, and the fact of our being all at home together precludes visitors. I suppose Rhondda is comparatively 'safe' despite the dense population...

The news about your financial prospects makes things more cheerful. Let's hope indeed that this wretched war does not come off!

I wonder what are the 'Welsh books' you have. I am to blame for not sending you the elementary primers which I promised to get. I will get them at the first opportunity, but there will be plenty of time again for you to dig into them.

Do send me your impressions of Betws-y-coed and district. I'm afraid I don't know much about it, although I once passed through on my way to Bangor. I can see that you will soon be showing me around my own country as you have shown London to me!

In a further (undated) letter, Gwyn says that his speech in Treharris went well:

My speech has been delivered and loudly acclaimed, but alas I am not sure whether it will affect the international situation.

The moon was very beautiful last night and it was probably more so in Betws-y-coed. There will be beautiful moons again. Let us hope we shall be soon together to enjoy them.

The next letter from Kate relates her experience of escaping to the mountains, and it includes her first written Welsh words.

You ask me how I like your mountains. It was a falling in love at the first glance and I blessed my quick resolution many a time already.

The first impression was: There is something like a German
'*Wald*', the Schwarzwald [the Black Forest], the Thüringerwald,
real aimless nature, the thing I had missed so much in the tidiness
of the lovely English countryside. As soon as possible I climbed
upwards, not very far though, to the Llyn Elsi with its splendid
view to over seven rows of mountains one behind the other with
heather, *Farnkraut* [fern] (what is the English word?) climbing
sheep like on old pictures of biblical stories.

At the lake I met two 'ladies' who asked me for the way and
were surprised that I was walking quite by myself. 'Are you not
afraid?' – 'Afraid? of what?' and I really meant it. No, I don't
mind being here for a while by myself. Once I felt lonely, that was
between the Somerville dons. But the mountains give some kind
of relation in a strange way...

In town you have many aims and no aim, you are torn into
different directions knowing by yourself that you may sit down as
well and do nothing. Here you find at once one very definite aim:
you must climb... There is something else as well: the hills have
something sociable: you never get to know them completely. Even
going to the same place again and again: flowers change, the clouds
have different shapes, different animals are crawling and flying
and climbing around you. You do not ask any longer: What is
the aim of life? Is it worth living? [She then says in German:] *One
enjoys existing, and yet one is not without thought. Existing is a joy in
itself, a blessing, something one experiences humbly with the whole body.
"Consider the lilies of the field, how they grow!"*

She then describes how she found herself amid the rocks,
thorns, ferns and slate walls, and tried to climb and jump. She
tore her stockings and her legs bled. Her bracelet and jacket were
ripped by a branch:

> I discovered that my jacket had gone! ... it was impossible for me
> to find it and I felt quite exhausted. And in the pocket was my
> 'Welsh made easy'. I was very angry with myself...
>
> A propos Welsh books. Besides the lost one I bought a small
> dictionary and a Bible at your Welsh shop in Charing-Cross Road.

Luckily enough I found in this house a number of children's
schoolbooks edited by D. J. Williams which will help me along.

Now to your or better our plans: I read on a Photo-shop today:
'Closed until noon on Monday the 28th unless Hitler interferes.'

So I say: So God will or unless Hitler interferes I propose the
following things:

Are you sure that the British Museum will be open so that you
can work there?

Will your brother-in-law be back?

In that case there are two possibilities: we might meet in Wales
at a place near Rhondda.

Or I may stay in London for a few days in a Hotel as I did
before.

I want to be back in Somerville today (Monday) fortnight.

I certainly want to see you before going back to Oxford...

Much love [She finishes the letter with her first words of
written Welsh:]

Yr wyf fi yn dy garu di, Gwyn, bob dydd a bob nos.

[I love you, Gwyn, every day and every night]

Yours

Käthe

In a letter on 24 August 1939, Gwyn explains again his feelings
about the war which was imminent. He considers all political
powers in Europe to be imperialist, and that democracy is of no
interest to them, unless the threat to democracy is likely to disturb
the influence of their own imperialism. (It is possible to adapt this
argument to the way in which the United States and Britain in
the 21st century have bombed the countries of the Middle East
and northern Africa under the guise of democracy, although the
real reason was political influence and gaining control of oil.)
Gwyn writes:

When you get this you will of course be in London, and I expect
we will be in the throes of the crisis. I have been worrying about
you also on this account. And London, alas! is not a good place at a
time like this.

You already know my ideas about the crisis. I don't think there is one single argument for not letting Germany have Danzig, and England will be completely mad if she will try to stop her. The present mood of the English Government seems to be that, although Hitler has won an undoubted triumph on the Russian front, yet we will show him that we intend sticking to our guns! Nothing more foolish or ridiculous could be imagined. It would be much better for England to admit that she is beaten and give way to the inevitable. If she goes to war, it will be simply to prevent German hegemony on a broad imperialist basis. The talk about 'democracy' is sheer bunkum, with Poland, Greece, and Turkey as chief allies. If Wales had her own government, she would without doubt take her stand with Holland, Sweden, Denmark etc. – which are real democracies. I am heartily sick of the blustering folly of the Big Powers, every single one of them.

On the last day of August Gwyn sends another letter. He is still working on his doctorate, but by now has accepted a teaching post in Porth County School, Rhondda, to start in September.

With regard to plans, the crisis is still uncertain and now rather worse, owing to naval mobilisation. If you are quite free in your movements and are prepared to come to the South, near Rhondda, I should advise Cardiff. From the point of view of safety, it will be not so good as in the lovely North, but it is easily accessible to me – a journey of an hour by train…

On the other hand, if there was a chance of the museum opening soon, I would prefer you to be with me in London, as the next fortnight or so is the only chance for me to do some work before school.

My brother-in-law is unfortunately back at Ilford, so that I can hardly suggest you staying there, though you must certainly visit. If the Museum continues to be closed, I think I shall try Oxford.

You see that everything depends on these infernal politicians… I leave the decision in your hands, and hope that things will favour our meeting very soon…

Have you a radio in your present place? If not, you can be thankful. The news is now on, and it sounds as black as hell. I am amused, and rather ashamed, that you have been amassing a Welsh library quite unassisted by me. And I was thrilled at that closing sentence! *Yr wyf fi'n dy garu di, Käthe, – bob nos, bob dydd, ac am byth!* [I love you, Käthe, – every night, every day, and for ever!] The news is getting worse and worse. Has everything got to be sacrificed because of these imperial ambitions of England and Germany?

Gwyn says in another letter that Stephen, his brother-in-law, the husband of his sister Augusta, had to go back to Ilford 'to be ready to evacuate his school-children. There seems a little hope internationally, but the universal "precautions" must be costing a great deal'.

Kate was still in Betws-y-coed on 1 September:

There the sun is shining on a blue sky after a thunderstorm early this morning. And this is the first day of the evacuation! I wonder how much the '*Völkerwanderung*' [emigration of people] will affect North Wales.

So many thanks for your notes every day that give me something to look forward to, quasi the backbone of my days, and just make me feel how much I would like to talk with you and to enjoy with you the beauties of your home country and to find a rest at the heavy breast of my satyr…

My Welsh exercises concern specially the Bible and the place names and I just begin to read Political Penguin books again. Last night it was: 'I was Hitler's Prisoner' which I finished reading at 1 o'clock in the morning. To-day, I fear, the same thing will happen for me with Garrat's: Mussolini's Roman Empire.

Again and again one feels compelled to understand the mechanism of all that is happening to us.

But the same day Kate hears news of the declaration of war on the radio, and writes another letter:

Things could not be worse. So I decided to go to Cardiff tomorrow morning with the train leaving here at 7.57... I should be extremely thankful if you could meet me at the station in Cardiff... I feel in an awful position though my father said a war would do away with Hitler and would be to be preferred to the present suffering.

On 2 September Gwyn writes to Kate, clearly without an inkling of how Hitler would, in time, set about eliminating the Jews.

Your first letter arrived at 11.10 a.m. (second post), your second at 4.00 p.m. (third post) so that it was impossible for me to meet you at Cardiff at either of the times you suggested. I could come tonight or tomorrow, but it would not be easy to find you by random search.

Things are still very black, but we have not yet given up hope. You will understand that England and her 'guarantees' have been many times consigned to hell at Bryn Hyfryd. [Bryn Hyfryd was his parents' home.] There are three of us here liable to conscription, but we are unanimously agreed that if we believed in fighting it all, we would prefer to support Germany, in the present case, than England. Leaving the régime aside, one has to admit the justice of the claims against Versailles. However, as none of us believes in fighting, we shall, if war comes, be shot, jailed or sent to concentration camps. Your reading of 'Penguin' books will not help you to appreciate this standpoint, for if I am not mistaken, they are all written from the standpoint of the English 'Left' – with emphasis on English!
...

My work has naturally suffered owing to the tension of these days. One wants to know what is to be or not to be. I am sorry to hear that you are distracted. Disgust and fury seem more prominent here. If England wants to secure the independence of nations, she needn't go as far as Poland, nor need she shed one drop of blood.

I have not seen you since August 11th! It does seem a long age ago, and many things have happened. The tides of love are as strong as ever and surge even stronger through yearning and long absence... To see you again is now the big thing...

On the same day Kate arrived at the Hampton Hotel, 15 Pembroke Terrace, Cardiff and writes from there:

Mon Dieu, Gwyn,
What a day! I left B-y-C in lovely sunshine and arrived here at 6.30 in pouring rain, because of the evacuation trains. Very interesting at one side, people were all very friendly and sociable, on the other hand a nightmare-like procession of mothers with babies from Liverpool slum quarters.

Here in Cardiff it was difficult to find a room, all full of A.R.P. people, they say. So I am glad to have found at last a nice but damp basement room with wet walls. *Gott strafe Hitler!!* [May God punish Hitler!!]

PART 3

IN THE
GRASP OF WAR

The experiences
of Erika Ledien during
the war

ERIKA WAS THE ONLY daughter of Hans and Erika, and was a little younger than the children of Paul and Kaethe Bosse. After her father had been forced to flee to Shanghai, she had to face a difficult situation at home. Her mother had no means to keep up the house, and they moved to Stettin, now in north-western Poland. Erika could not attend the secondary school there and it was then arranged for her to return to Wittenberg to stay with acquaintances. This was not easy, particularly as she'd witnessed *Kristallnacht* in the town.

At the same time, she could see that Paul Bosse, her uncle, was extremely successful at work and settled with his family, and it was difficult for her to come to terms with this compared to the fate of her family and her father. This is reflected in her account of her childhood.[1]

When she was a member of the playgroup she looked forward to going to the primary school, to meet other children and learn to read and write, sing and draw. But it wasn't her parents who would take her to school, but their friends. Her own parents were afraid there would be animosity towards her if they took her. Erika received the traditional large bag of sweets given to children on their first day of school and she was happy. But the initial happiness did not last.

School could be uncomfortable. The first teacher she had was

Erika Viezens (formely Ledien) in Munich, 2011

an old, kind gentleman, but then a new teacher came, and he was one to be feared. The 'yellow police', as he called the cane, stood in a cupboard with an open door. Children who misbehaved were hit on their hands, and others had to stand for a while in the corner, facing the wall. Unfortunately the school yard stank with the smell from the toilets.

He parents had tried to get her into a small private school in Wittenberg, but because of the restrictions inflicted on the family, this had proved difficult. Erika notes:

Quite soon I started to feel that I was 'different' to my friends in class. After many children had been asked about their home, my turn came, I had to stand in front of the class, but I couldn't say anything about my home, as the teacher described me in a way that incensed me and said a lot of negative things about me... He said I was unfriendly, that I was unwilling to help, that I did not share, that I told lies and so on. The class was completely quiet. I told only Mother about this... How could she explain to me the spirit of the time? I was only eight years old and already extremely disappointed.

At home I faced difficulties when playing. The mothers of two children in the street had prohibited them from playing with me...

For one thing I would often be invited to children's birthday parties... Many children would come together, we had fun, we would beat drums, sing, also usually a chocolate marshmallow and choco, sometimes potato salad and sausages... But gradually my family feared that I wouldn't be invited any more, and when I met children and their mothers on the street, they would cross to the other side. The other children had piano lessons, or flute – but children of Jewish descent couldn't have music lessons... However I was completely unmusical... But I could write dictation with fewer mistakes and quicker than the rest. I knew as many names of flowers as Helgard, the best in the class. Why did I then have to stand last in the row on the school yard when the children's names were called?

Erika was in her element in her parents' company, especially her father, and he encouraged her interest in languages. It was the warmth of her relationship with her father that made it difficult for her to cope when he had to leave the country without much warning.

I could count up to one hundred in English. My father would travel to Berlin and learn Spanish and then English. He would read 'Winnie the Pooh' to me. He was a lovely man! I was allowed to stand on his shoes and he would walk me through the room; in the park I would run under his coat, which was green on the outside and red on the inside, and was comfortable and warm. He would always bring me lovely things, a pencil, with one side red and the other blue... a kaleidoscope which showed a world of wonder, a telephone for the doll's house, a small Christmas tree, which I later took with me to Frau Schmidt, to whom I had to go when Dad was in Shanghai and Mum in Dessau.

Her father's flight to Shanghai after his release from Buchenwald affected the family greatly, especially as his wife was in Dessau, some 25 miles from Wittenberg, looking after an aunt who was ill.

A part of the family's assets had been turned into money and we had to pay the 'Reichfluchtsteuer' – a tax for escaping from the country. He wasn't allowed to take a lot of money with him on the journey. Mum had no income. She decided to turn the one family house, which my father had transferred to me, into a two family house, and rented it then to an industrial concern. She made the large garage into a place to keep her furniture, and she took valuable objects to her father in Stettin. He lived as a widower with a maid in a house that my mother had built as an investment on her father's land and which was in a quiet area of villas. In the parent's house my mother lived with her brother and wife and their two children, around my age.

When I was taken to my grandfather, I took for granted that the cousins who lived next door could play with me. At the start, I could do that, but when my uncle had to fight, the aunt prohibited me from doing anything with her children. When I registered for the secondary school in 1941, she showed there my 'non-Aryan' ancestry. Although there were no definite rules, I was not allowed to go to school, it was suddenly 'overcrowded'.

In Wittenberg my mother made sure that I had education in the Lyceum, 'Katharinen-Oberschule für Mädchen' – a secondary school for girls. After Easter 1941 I was taken to Frau Schmidt, an elderly widow who had been one of Paul Bosse's patients... She lived in humble circumstances in a flat arranged in three rooms with a living kitchen in the roof of her parents' house. She supplemented her husband's pension who had died young through renting. In the room next to mine was the thirty-year-old secretary of the 'Winter School', who came from Flämming and who drove home each weekend. She often came with eggs, butter and a chicken now and again, which enhanced the food provision considerably. I had a room with a comparatively small window, which was rather dark and the furniture darkened the place further. Everything was old-fashioned and I longed for my airy children's room. I had my doll's pram from home and some small things, and an artificial Christmas tree that my father had brought me.

I didn't like this living kitchen at all, and was not fond of the bed sofa in the kitchen. The bathroom, without a window and without a washbasin, was not nice... Frau Schmidt was a very devout lady. She went to church regularly... she would go to funerals, whether near or far, which she got to know about through the *Wittenberger Tageblatt*. She would also take care of a row of graves, too many for my liking because I had to go with her often to the graveyard which was far out – she went on her bicycle. I had to run alongside carrying a small rake. She would

water and tidy the grave of her parents, her husband, her son (who
had been a school friend of Fritz, so born in 1915), the grave of the
old Bosse family, the old Ledien family. When I was at my wits'
end, she would then go to the 'Grave of Onkel Willi' (my father's
big brother, who had died of diphtheria when he was three or four
years old, a little before the turn of the century) and to 'Peterchen'
(who died of tetanus, Dolly Maier-Bosse's son).

... Frau Schmidt opposed the Nazis. She was very orderly,
clean, frugal, and she was always petty bourgeois, bossy, and not
suitable for a girl as little as I was at the time – ten-and-a-half when
I went to her. There were hardly any books in her home and she
disapproved of my moods. As no-one was allowed to come to the
flat, I was always on my own with her and so I read a lot, often
under the blankets with a torch.

I always obtained the batteries from Knubben, Günther's wife
from Sweden, whose flat was only twenty minutes away on foot.
I liked being with her. She was comparatively young, 16 years
older than me, and she had two small girls who were born in 1938
(Ingrid) and 1940 (Kristina). I was allowed to be at her wedding
with Günther. They had celebrated in Bosse's house at that time,
which Onkel Paul, after having to give up his work as senior
doctor of Wittenberg Hospital, had turned into a private clinic for
operations and women's illnesses (and births). The table had been
put in a wide hall, and I would sit with Eva-Monika, who was five
years older than I, and Hänschen Bosse, who was in his teens at
the time, and I remember that we had wine. That did not agree
with me and it suited my father to leave the meal early, and I was
allowed to go to bed, as I also had whooping cough.

My father often had heated arguments with his brother-in-
law [Paul Bosse], with whom he had had an uneasy relationship.
He had known him since he was a small child, and he used to
play with him – he was six years older – on the piece of land
that stretched behind the parents' house, and he was often given
a small pencil by him as a present. On the one hand this pleased
him a lot, but on the other he reacted strongly against his over-
patronising manner, and so things remained throughout his life.

My father was amazed by the numerous talents of his

brother-in-law, and he appreciated them, but he condemned his very authoritarian and patriarchal behaviour, which forced my father's sister, in his opinion, to play an unworthy role. I could see that Tante Kaethe, who was a year younger than my father, was always dependent on her husband, always serving him, very much in his shadow, according to his wish.

He arranged his life according to his needs, he would follow his inclinations and was keenly interested, for example, in new technical things, and would buy things in Leipzig Fair [a large annual technical fair] for the clinic, the home, the farm. He collected stamps on a large scale, taking a whole room to do that, and no-one under any circumstances was to interrupt him when he was in the middle of studying and arranging. He was a keen cinemagoer, and he had his own seat in the Central Theater, a modern cinema by his home. On rare occurrences, Tippen [Dolly's first son] (his eldest grandson whom he completely worshipped) and I could go with him to see a film.

He was especially fond of plants, and had a glasshouse in the garden, and it was quite in keeping with his interests when he bought a farm for Fritz, his youngest son, after he had to give up his studies in the secondary school because of the increasing anti-Semitism, so that the son could be kept busy with this. He obtained modern equipment for this farm, including machinery, which would certainly not be profitable for such a small business. He built hot and cold houses, and would grow vegetables which appeared exotic for us at the time, such as paprika and melons. The produce of this farm, with early salads, cucumbers, tomatoes and so on, was very skilful and was sent to the kitchen of the clinic, and they were a considerable attraction there, and the arrangement of the kitchen ensured that these looked attractive.

Wives from nearby farming areas or from the world of business liked going to the private clinic for women, and it had a good reputation because of its atmosphere, thanks to the friendly care of the Catholic sisters from Koblenz and their excellent cooking skills from the Rhine region. The eagerness of Opa [Paul Bosse] to keep stock, for which he used half the annexe, was a great help in the years of scarcity during the war, and this was a solid source of ingredients for the kitchen sisters.

Opa took pride in boasting about his treasures. He would take us through the rooms with all the shelves, where he kept things that we no longer available: raisins, almonds, cocoa, coffee, jam, and a wealth of other materials, and raffia. When Opa was in good spirits, he was seen to be generous. The family, which was growing in size, would have some of the produce. Dark blue cotton with white dots was eventually to be seen on all the female members of the family, even as far as Dessau, on my mother. It was forced on Itti [Brigitte, the daughter of Walter Mannchen and Leonore] and me. The material was practical and pretty, but in Wittenberg it had an unfortunate condemnatory effect, as it was a sign that we belonged to the family.

The raffia was a source of pure joy. We had done so many things from it, presents for various occasions, mainly shopping bags, which were no longer to be seen in the shops. They were lined with oilcloth – also from Opa's stock! – and these were greatly appreciated by the family.

We spent many hours with Oma [Kaethe Bosse] producing these. Eventually we became adept at producing 'card pockets'. There was a special demand for these wallets to hold the innumerable food cards which were so important for living in every family. For every member of the family one would have new cards every month: cards for bread, white bread and cakes, meat, eggs, processed food, vegetables, potatoes, smoking products, and 'points cards' for textiles. The rations varied in size. Jews would not get some cards, for example no meat cards and no smoking cards. The smoking cards were greatly valued as exchange cards.

The card wallets were used more and more. A new one would be badly needed after a year at most. We were never therefore without ideas for presents. Oma had received a 'zig-zag foot' from the fair in Leipzig for her sewing machine and she used it enthusiastically. If it was at all possible to use it, the zig-zag sewing pattern was used. All the work would start on the spur of the moment and would be finished quickly and skilfully, with a wealth of ideas and also with a hot needle. I liked seeing Oma, who was welcoming and full of life and who appeared to me to be optimistic compared to my mother, although she was not able to hide her worry and pain…

I still remember vividly the day of 20 July 1944. I was in Dessau, where my mother was looking after Tante Lore, who was ill with TB, and her family. Apart from Tante Lore the family also included Onkel Walter (Walter Mannchen, a chemist in Aken/ Elbe in the IG paint factory which was important for the war, after he had been forced to give up his career in Göttingen University because of Tante Lore), and two children, Brigitte (born 1936) and Justus (born 1939). The family lived in a leafy area, a suburb to the west, in a house for four families. The landlord was a grumpy metal worker, but he was without fault politically, and had retired. In the flat next to him was Herr Krebs, a talented little plump man, who had been a coal merchant but who went bankrupt.

He had let his wife run the business, a little woman who was just as plump. His hair was completely black, and he looked as if he had been picked up from an anti-Jewish propaganda leaflet, and he had managed to get an important job: he was the chief defence officer against air raids in Dessau. He was unpleasantly important, throwing doors open when he would rush to his office, and ran around in his grey air defence uniform. Herr Krebs was definitely a Nazi, but he sympathised with our family. If enemy aeroplanes approached he would give two rings on the phone before the warning alarm as a sign for us. We then had more time. Tante Lore, by the way, was allowed to go into the air raid cellar, which Jews were not otherwise allowed to do.

On 20 July 1944 the phone rang many times, and Herr Krebs was agitated on the other end of the line: someone had tried to kill Hitler, and Hitler had survived. Tante Lore and Mum were immediately very afraid that people would come to search the house and that they would be arrested, and they went to fetch the boxes of letters that had been written by friends at the time of the plotting against Tante Lore's parents and her sister before Tante Lore's parents were sent out of the country. Friends and those who knew them had expressed their sympathy and now they shouldn't be put in any danger. Mum and Tante Lore read parts of the

wonderful letters once again and burnt them. That lasted hours.
They were frightened by a phone call from Wittenberg from
Frau Schmidt, who said that all the Bosse family had 'gone on a
journey', that is, that they had all been arrested...

The 20th of July was still a holiday for me, but an important
one, as this was the last day of my school term. I wanted to go to
school again after the holiday, but it was explained to me that they
didn't want to see me again and, in spite of my mother's protests,
that remained the situation. The head teacher was so threatening
that Mum was afraid that the same thing could happen to me
as happened to the sons of my father's colleague, Dr Simson of
Jessen. Dr Simson had been an officer in the First World War
and in 1918 he lost an arm, but he had taken his life in order to
protect his Aryan wife and their mixed-race sons. But they did not
succeed. The two grammar school pupils were sent to a 'work and
education camp'.

Mum took me as a maid to the house of a deaconess in Dessau,
which included a large number of buildings, with a mothers'
home, and old people's home, a children's home, a hospital and
a sheltered home. I was supposed to have a place in the sheltered
home, which was a home for 'fallen girls'. Mum had managed to
arrange that I would work in the day in the deaconess's home and
I could go home in the evening.

At home there was a four-room flat, where we were now three
adults and three children.

It was not far to the deaconess's house, which was in the same
street as the Bauhaus, about 15 to 20 minutes for me. I had to be
in the service in the morning, the deaconess and the workers of
the house gathered in the mothers' home, a red brick building of
the turn of the century. What gave me a fright when I saw the
deaconess on the first day, was that she was wearing the Party's
badge on her dress! But I had no contact with this sister and I had
no political trouble...

They would pray every morning and sing hymns, but the
quarrelling and the conflict, the competition and the envy among
the sisters was fierce.

Food was one of the main disputes among the sisters as well

as fear of the air raids that became more frequent and so they wanted to claim their own place. Improving the food situation wasn't worth thinking about. Then one day a miracle occurred: just as in a fable a huge number of people took to the streets with pots, buckets, jugs and we found out that a fountain of treacle had sprung: the silos of the sugar factory had been hit by bomb fragments. Now sweet smelling streams were flowing from the many holes. At the deaconess's house I had to fetch a bucket and an old shaky hand-cart from the stable, and then a girl from the sheltered home and I went to the popular fountain. The nearer we got, the stronger was the smell and the earth became damp and slippery. We thought that we had been cunning when we found that the railway tracks led straight past the silos where the treacle was flowing into a flat lake...

We were in luck. We reached the holes in the metal container made by the grenade fragments, from which the sweet liquid flowed in streams. Our buckets were quickly full and after a little difficulty on the way back we reached the deaconess's house, but we weren't warmly welcomed there, because in the meantime someone had come around with a megaphone warning against eating the treacle because it was very poisonous and that it must be thrown away. Thrown away, where? In the toilets? The substance was too sticky for that. After a few days we threw it in the garden, thoroughly disappointed.

At home Onkel We [Walter] had been sent on a bike to get some of the 'miracle treacle'. He had gone with Justus, who was five years old and whose shoes had become completely stuck, but they did get two buckets of treacle. We were now faced at home with the problem of getting rid of the sticky substance. And how would we get our shoes clean again? All our effort was in vain, it was awful because we could not possibly get new shoes. At best we could get ration sandals or a cloth shoe with wooden soles. These were painful on the feet and one would get blisters... Mum had heard about the existence of a shoe exchange centre. I hoped I would be able to change my shoes, which had become too small, for bigger shoes, but unfortunately an air raid had demolished the centre and had burnt my shoes.

When I became a member of the Church in March 1945 I was given shoes by my mother, one whole size too small! But the shoes weren't the only things that were too small, my dress was also too tight. I had borrowed it from Tante Lisa, Onkel Walter Mannchen's little sister. Quite unreasonably, with the war almost at an end, the requirement to dress up for confirmation was still in force: a dark suit for boys, dark dresses for girls. I had a year and a half of confirmation lessons, but I learnt almost nothing. Knowledge of the Bible = nil. Lost time! The ceremony took place in the town church in Wittenberg, but it was quite short, as an air raid alarm had interrupted proceedings... we had coffee at the flat which Günther and Edith (Knubben) had left in Lutherstraße 14a. Günther was in the camp in Zöschen, and Knubben on her way to Sweden. The Swedish government had ordered its citizens to leave Germany and to travel home. Knubben at the time was with Ingrid and Kristina in Aumühle near Hamburg...

Early in the night there was a new alarm, and we heard the bomber aeroplanes roaring and eventually explosions in the

Erika Viezens (centre) reminiscing with her family during a family reunion, Munich, 2011

distance. After the alarm, when we had to wait in the cellar, we could see the red sky in the west – where was the fire? The next day we wanted to go to Dessau (37 kilometres away); the railway was available, but only as far as Roßlau, this side of the Elbe. People in the train reported that Dessau had been bombed, and one could see the black-red sky, and scared people. My mother joined a group that was going towards the Elbe, and there, after some waiting, we squeezed into a crowded boat and we walked the seven or eight kilometres through fields towards Dessau. The air became greyer and greyer, full of smoke. We walked past houses that had been burnt; we saw ruins, some still burning. There was rubble, smashed glass, fire bombs, disoriented people. We were on tenterhooks; would we find our house once again? As we came to the 'Seven Columns' at the far end of Georgengarten, and reached Ziebigker Straße, we hardly dared to look around the corner. We ran, we saw demolished houses everywhere, but our house was still standing! We stumbled in, everyone was alive! They were all busy clearing the debris and putting cardboard or something similar instead of glass in the windows… on the oven soup had been cooked for all, it tasted like a feast. We could hardly believe that we had been saved, although three-quarters of the town had been destroyed on 7 March 1945…

Another two years went by before her father Hans could return to the family. Erika's mother had insisted that she should grow her hair until her father returned:

For years we didn't know if he was still alive. But during the autumn of 1947, in Wutta by Eisenach, my mother was able to present her daughter to my father with her hair not having been cut (though I ran at once then to the hairdresser…) However the plaited hair did not help her father to recognise his daughter. He was in the quarantine section, standing in front of his wife and the three little children, he pointed at Itti [Brigitte], who was at the time eleven years old, and asked, 'Is it her?' I was awfully sad.

The wealth of Rhondda

B EFORE COMING TO WALES Kate had wished for a more challenging life, and also marriage. But, this had hardly included a desire to change language and nationality, but since starting her relationship with Gwyn she was already developing an interest in Welsh. The courtship had been sudden and swift, and by the middle of August 1939 both agreed that they would marry. As the war started, and with the danger that those from Germany could be interred, she and Gwyn married hastily. How would a mining village in Rhondda welcome a foreign girl who was now one of the enemy?

It became difficult to correspond with relatives in Germany, but some letters could be sent and received via Sweden. Kate took advantage of her connection with Stina Anderson of Landskrona, Sweden, who was a cousin of Edith, Günther's husband. This was the only way Kate could receive information about her family in Germany, and she had already started writing to her in English in 1939 after returning from Holland, where she had met her father, brother and nephew:

> Dear Stina,
>
> So many thanks for your letter which I received just now. Please pardon me for writing in English. But the letters abroad are censored and they pass quickly like that. I think the best thing will be if you write to Wittenberg a report about the things I tell you…
>
> I have not heard from home since my father and Fritz and Tippen left me in Holland and therefore I did not write to them as

I was afraid that it might be dangerous for them to have relations with England.

Kate then talks about her new life in Wales, and says why she has to get married so suddenly:

Now you will be surprised. Because of the war I have married very quickly. It happened quite dramatically. So now I am the wedded wife of Gwyn Griffiths, school teacher in Porth and formerly student of Egyptology in Oxford. We're living with his parents (and at the moment with two brothers and one sister) in a very pleasant hilly spot in South Wales and while writing I have a look at the mountains through the window. It is the same man about whom I have told my father in Holland.

At the beginning of the war (I was in North Wales at the time) Gwyn asked me to stay with his family, which I did. They were all very nice but it was sure that we would have much difficulty if we asked them to allow us to marry. So we did it secretly and announced the result only afterwards and after the first shock was over they are really very nice indeed and almost proud of our deed.

It is hardly necessary to tell that I have in Gwyn a husband with whom I harmonize almost in every direction and it is a very nice feeling to know that he is proud of me.

Now I have to learn Welsh as people here prefer speaking Welsh to speaking English. I shall write more soon. But I want you to assure my parents that I am much happier than it is right in war times and that my life is as dramatically romantic as ever...

Gwyn later explained the need to marry so soon:

There was an element of haste in the wedding on 13 September 1939, and that was so because the bride, as a German, faced the fate of being kept in an internment camp under the War regulations. The honeymoon was spent in Oxford. We were staying in Wellington Square. There was no marriage feast, but we had a personally warm dinner in Somerville College with the Principal Helen Darbishire. Professor Gunn (Egyptology) also came to see us, and gave a present and congratulations.[2]

Gwyn and Kate Bosse-Griffiths on their wedding day

On 26 February, Stina wrote to Kate to say that her parents had not received the letters sent to them through the Red Cross. She said that Günther her brother was now fighting in the army but had been taken ill, and that Fritz was also deployed in the army.

On 4 March Kate answered her letter; she was now living with her new husband at 14 St Stephens's Avenue, Pentre, Rhondda, and the letter includes one of Kate's first impressions of her new life:

Now, I really have got a home of my own. It is only a few houses away from the house of Gwyn's parents, right up on the hill, at the foot of the mountains and when the sun is shining it is very beautiful here. The house we bought from an old man with the furniture, which of course is not quite new either. But we are papering some of the rooms and got a big new bookshelf and my mother-in-law helps me find the right people to do things and tells me how to do Welsh cooking. Gwyn is teaching at a school in Porth and is living here in Pentre, of course.

From time to time people ask me to give lectures or to take the chair in some singing festivals and so I feel very happy as I see that they like to hear me speaking in public.

Oma will feel glad to hear that we have got plenty of food. How much I wished that they could come and see everything themselves.

I got a letter from Onkel Hans about a week ago, but by mistake the censor had put a soldier's letter to his wife into the envelope and so I do not know what Onkel Hanne wanted to tell me...

Tell them my love and say that they shall try and carry through in these hard times and that they shall not lose confidence, that there is an end to every evil if we only wait long enough.

Then Kate managed to get a letter from her parents, through Stina. She heard that Günther was still ill in the army hospital, and that the family was worried about him.

More of Kate's impressions of Rhondda were expressed in two different publications. In the November/December 1940 issue of *Heddiw* [Today], a new Welsh literary magazine, there appeared a sonnet by Kate about Moel Cadwgan, the mountain which rises above Pentre:

> *Gwêl modd y cwyd y rhesi tai o'r cwm,*
> *Yn benllwyd, fel ar bererinol daith;*
> *Tu hwnt mae'r hen fynyddoedd beilchion, llwm,*
> *Llwythog gan lo, er hyn, trystfawr gan waith.*
> *Yn igam-ogam ar ddibalmant lwybr*
> *Dringasom yma i fangre hardd yr haul,*
> *A rhywrai odditanom yn ddiwybr*
> *Yn cloddio'r mwyn disgleirddu er eu traul.*
> *Gorffwysa'r ŵyn ar hyd y glaswellt ir*
> *Megis pe daethent o ryw santaidd lun.*
> *Ac fel yr esgyrn sydd yn gannaid draw,*
> *Olion crwydredig ddefaid a fu'n hir*
> *Heb ofal bugail, felly i lygaid un*
> *Mae gwynion gerrig-feddau'r gladdfa wrth law.*

See how the rows of valley houses rise,
Grey headed, as if on a pilgrim journey;
Beyond are the old, proud, bare mountains,
Heavy with coal, in spite of this, noisy with work.
We climbed on a zig-zag pavementless path
To a beautiful spot in the sun,
And some ones skyless below us
Were digging the bright black ore at their cost.
The lambs rest on the green grass
As if they had come from some holy picture.
And just as the bones that are blanched yonder,
The remains of wandering sheep who had been so long
Without shepherd, so to one person's eyes
Are the white gravestones of the nearby graveyard.

Although Kate had started learning Welsh by now, it is impossible to imagine that she could have mastered the language sufficiently to write poems at this stage. Gwyn told me that the process was one of co-composing at that time. Kate would form her poem in German, but they would then co-translate into Welsh. It is certain that this happened later on too when Kate started writing stories to be published in Welsh. In the case of this poem, it is clear that it is a translation.

Two years later, Kate prepared a quarter-of-an-hour's talk for the Home Service of the BBC, which was broadcast on 27 October 1942, under the title *I Married a Welshman*. In it she mentions the Welsh language and she presents her early impressions of Rhondda.

> I saw the first written Welsh in one of my most desperate periods as a refugee when I received the holiday address of Amabel Williams Ellis [she was the wife of the architect Clough Williams-Ellis, of Portmeirion fame, and who belonged to a movement that gave assistance to refugees]. I copied it out as what was to me a sequence of meaningless letters, 'Plas Brondanw, Llanfrothen Station, Penrhyndeudraeth, North Wales'. It was in Oxford that I heard the first spoken Welsh, when my husband told me: '*Rwy'n dy garu di*', which seemed to me then rather a complicated way of saying 'I love you'.
>
> Already on my first visit to Rhondda, on the way to see my future family-in-law, I fell in love with the Welsh mountains. It was love at first sight which has not diminished since. In the train I looked through the window, fascinated by the beauty of the bare, sharply cut hills which enclosed us. What pictures they recalled to my mind! The bare hills of the Hymettos Mountains near Athens; an afternoon in the Bavarian Alps, when I stood on the top of the Brauneck looking down on a sea of clouds; morning sunshine in the Egyptian desert... 'Don't you find them ugly?' – my husband interrupted my day-dreams. 'Ugly?... What?' – 'Those black coal tips and especially those holes high up there.' Only with difficulty could my inexperienced eye distinguish the row of caves which

hung around the neck of the mountains like a string of black beads. 'The colliers cut their own coal there during the Big Strike,' he explained... Then I heard for the first time those fateful words 'The Big Strike', which has become almost a means of dating in the valleys, just as in England they would say 'in the year of the Coronation'...

Kate then mentions an occasion when Pennar Davies, the poet, scholar and theologian who was a college friend of Gwyn at Cardiff and Oxford, came to call on them at midnight:

A familiar voice was heard, and wet in spite of the dry night, with dirt all over his best suit and completely exhausted, a poet friend from a neighbouring valley came in. In a fashion which I know prevailed with the Greek Homeric heroes, the first thing I offered him was a hot footbath; after that the cup of tea which is given in Rhondda at any time of day and night to every visitor, and a quickly prepared supper. Only then did we ask him, again in accordance with the ancient Greek code of manners, where he came from that night... He had tried to take a short cut and had lost his way in a starless night to such an extent that he was nearly drowned in a mountain pool. After going round in a circle once or twice he decided to keep his direction by walking towards a searchlight. After hours of stumbling about, he arrived at last at a place which was many miles away from us. He did not finish his 'wanderings' without meeting a Home Guard who took him for one of those tall fair-haired German parachutists. Luckily enough he did not shoot him at sight, but only asked him for his identity card.

I said with intention that I followed the old Greek code of manners in receiving our guest, because one thing that strikes me again and again is the similarity between some of the Welsh ways of thinking and living and those of the ancient Greeks. Have you ever seen how a Welsh mother throws around her body the big shawl in which she holds her child safely and warmly? The beauty of the fall of its folds reminds one of the grace of Greek and Roman statues.

Kate then expresses amazement at the rich life of Rhondda, and at how she was readily accepted there:

Did you ever hear a Welsh non-conformist congregation discuss the merits of a sermon? Only in Wales did I learn to understand why the rhetoric of Greek and Roman orators received so much praise... But only when you have taken part in a poetic, dramatic or singing competition in one of the local Eisteddfodau – or even in the annual National Eisteddfod – do you know how near the Welsh spirit is to that competitive spirit which, in Athens in the fifth and fourth century B.C., founded our European culture...

The eagerness of the Welsh to appreciate knowledge gave me one of the greatest surprises in my new life... I kept in my mind the popular prejudice that a real woman should not be a 'blue-stocking' and that a girl who has the bad luck to be an 'intellectual' should at least try and hide it as well as possible. But even before I had time to settle down to married life my husband's family urged me on: 'Surely you will give an address to our Young People's Society?'... A new life full of activities opened itself for me, quite different from the monotonous provincial life of which some friends had warned me. Rhondda seemed to be teeming with societies, most of them connected with the Non-conformist chapels... Adult schools, sisterhoods, Young People's Societies, Unemployed Clubs: they sensed that I had something to offer them even before I had realized it myself...

I felt as if I had started a new life; and really, like a growing child I am now trying to master a new language – the Welsh language. I learn Welsh not only in order to get to know the riches of the Welsh literature... but in order to come nearer to the soul of the Welsh... Every attempt of mine to express myself in Welsh was greeted with a smiling satisfaction which was already a reward of its own, and urged on through this smile I hastened to get over that stage when people stopped talking Welsh as soon as I entered the room and changed to English, to show that they did not have any secrets in front of me...

The Russian nobility have rightly been praised for the grace with which they took manual work as porters and waitresses when exile forced them to do so, but in Wales I found a nation where working people have the culture and dignity of princes.

There were other worries during 1940. Peter, the son of her sister Dolly, died after cutting himself with a knife, and the family had not realized that the poison would prove fatal. Kate herself was expecting her first baby, and Gwyn was finishing his doctorate thesis. Kate told Stina in November:

> I feel very well indeed without being sick or any greater discomfort than being just a little more tired than usual.
>
> I went to the clinic last Friday, and they found everything O.K. But nevertheless we decided that I shall have the baby in hospital to be quite sure...
>
> Now I started to knit little baby things out of the lovely Scotch baby wool. I even finished my first pullover for Gwyn and have learned how to knit gloves. Beside that I am writing poems and stories for a Welsh magazine, and Gwyn and I are reading and writing together... Our food is as good as ever: fruit, full corn bread, milk, meat, etc, cereals in the morning...

However, in April 1942, when the baby came, it was stillborn, suffering from hydrocephalus. Pennar Davies, who was still known as Bill Davies at that time, wrote to them in Welsh:

> I'm deeply sorry to hear about the misfortune this morning. It is an awful disappointment for you, I know, but we must give thanks that Käthe herself is getting along so well. She is safe – that is the most important thing, and I'm very joyful for that. It is sad and sorry that a small life comes to an end like this, but that is part of the secret of life. May she have an easy passage to the land of the spirit.
>
> You and Käthe have enough time to have a child again... My mother had two dead babies before giving birth to my eldest sister, and she then had four children which is a great credit for her on the whole. It tells you: Do not despair on all accounts. It is good that Käthe is still so brave in spite of the disappointment. As you say she and you will also have more time now for making

literature, art and philosophising. And I'm sure that you will have a lovable baby before very long. Don't ever give up...

Bil

★ ★ ★

The war effort called for soldiers. As in the case of most young people of conscription age, Gwyn would be expected to join the armed forces. That is what his brother Gwilym did some time later. The young men of Moreia chapel, where Gwyn's father Robert Griffiths was a minister, were joining the army to fight in a war which could be claimed to be an honourable one. Gwilym felt that he too had to join and signed up for the air force. But he could not stomach the bayonet practice, with sacks being used as people, and he could not see himself as a part of a system that encouraged killing. Instead of passing mathematics tests etc. that would have enabled him to qualify eventually as a pilot, Gwilym deliberately decided to do badly. As a result of failing one test after another, he spent his time scrubbing floors instead of preparing to fly.

Then he decided to run away. He spent the war years hiding from the authorities, but secretly managed to visit home. He used the identity papers of Pennar Davies's father and went to Oxford, taking on the role of a student. It was during this period that he wrote a long essay on Guiseppe Mazzini, the Italian nationalist who led the efforts to secure Italian independence. Police in Rhondda were constantly on his trail and his acquaintances had to deny all knowledge of his whereabouts, although he was already courting Edna Lewis of Ton Pentre. He spent periods in Capel-y-ffin, in Monmouthshire, in a monastery established by Father Ignatius near Llanthony Priory. He also became a student in Liverpool, and was almost caught when his brother Dafydd sent him a letter using his real name. At the end of the war Gwilym walked into the Scotland Yard office in London to admit having run away from the armed forces and spent some months in prison.

Gwyn, on the other hand, as his letters to Kate demonstrate, opposed the war. In June 1940, he had to present a case to the local tribunal for registering as a conscientious objector.

Pennar Davies gave him advice in a letter dated 2 September 1940:

> Remember to talk firmly, quietly and courteously, and with conviction. If they ask the question about a madman attacking your wife or your sister, reply negatively that you will not kill a man in any circumstances, and add that the great enemy of your wife and her sisters and every man and child in the world is war! Say that the only way to conquer Nazism and every other oppression is passive resistance, say with emphasis that you are willing to face prison or the firing squad. Regarding the RAMC [Royal Army Medical Corps] your argument is that it is part of the army. They will say that it is a special, humanitarian, Christian part! Then you must say that in spite of that, it is a part of the army and as you believe that all armies must be abolished, you cannot join. But you know all this, and much more! Forgive these advisory notes. And best wishes. It will greatly surprise me if you get less than unconditional discharge.

Gwyn prepared his application on Christian grounds, and presented it in Welsh:

> Religious conviction is the only ground for my objection.
> I believe passionately that war contravenes the will of God as it is made evident in Jesus Christ and his Gospel. In its aims and means and results, war, in my view, utterly contradicts the way of Christ; and because I am trying to follow this Christ, I promised to abstain completely from war. I am thankful for the opportunity to testify like this. The way which Christ preached during his life, and walked as well, that is the way I try to preach and walk. I cannot take part in war and be faithful to this ideal. I feel at the same time, of course, that opposing in this manner is not my only duty, but to

A certificate releasing Gwyn from military service

be a medium for promoting the spirit and the desire for real peace. This principle has had an important place in my life. It influenced extensively, for example, my political belief. I believe in Christian nationalism, and in freedom for Wales. I have urged many times publicly, in word and in writing, that non-violent means should be the way.

The principle has never been strange to me. I am the son of Reverend Robert Griffiths, a minister with the Welsh Baptists in Pentre, Rhondda, and I am now a deacon in Moreia church, Pentre, and a Sunday School teacher. I have been active with the peace cause in the universities of Wales, Liverpool and Oxford, and I can show a certificate testifying my activities with the Peace Ballot in 1934. I was one of the first to join, in 1936, the Mudiad Heddychwyr Cymru [The Welsh Peace Pledge Movement] started in *Y Brython* [The Britton] by the Reverends J. P. Davies and J. W. Jones. In my denomination I praised the leadership of people like Dr E. K. Jones, and I seriously undertook the peace resolution of the Union in Rhosllanerchrugog.

I have been a lay preacher, for some years, with the Welsh

Baptists. In August 1939 I had the honour of addressing the
Welsh Baptist Union in Treharris. At that occasion I expressed my
conviction that the Church should not compromise in its attitude
towards war. Since then nothing has happened to change this
conviction. I am opposing as I cannot do otherwise.

During the hearing Gwyn said that he opposed non-combatant
activities, but that he would not oppose working on the land.
His application succeeded, and he was granted unconditional
discharge.

Arresting
Günther and Fritz

FROM HIS EARLY DAYS, Fritz, Kate's brother, had been a keen member of the youth movement in Germany. In spite of political difficulties in Germany, and the way in which his family was being treated, when the call came from the *Wehrmacht*, the army, Fritz, Günther and Georg, Dolly's husband, all enlisted. In one incident during the fighting, Günther was wounded in the chest. Being of Jewish extraction did not seem to be a problem for the military services at the start of the war, but by 1940 the three of them had been dismissed from the army. The note in the military card stated that they were not very dependable.

By that time Fritz was engaged to Sophie, a local girl of German descent. The Gestapo told him that he had to break off the engagement.

In Günther's case, the wound he suffered was an excuse for the Wittenberg branch of the Nazi Party to refuse him permission to continue with his medical work.

One heroic aspect of the period in Germany was the way in which many opposed Hitler. Some of the opposition was on pacifist grounds, but there were many attempts to kill Hitler by his adversaries at different times during the war. The attempt by Stauffenberg and his fellow conspirators on 20 July 1944 is the most notable. This has been recorded in the American film *Valkyrie* (2008). In Wales, the account was described forcefully

Günther Bosse   Fritz Bosse

by dramatist Saunders Lewis in his play *Brad* [Treason], which was performed for the first time during the National Eisteddfod in Ebbw Vale in 1958.

In his play, Saunders Lewis discusses the honour of German army officers who had realised that Hitler was a great evil. Philipp von Boeselager, one of the officers involved in the 1944 assasination attempt on the Führer, gives his personal account in his memoir, *Valkyrie, the Plot to Kill Hitler*.[3]

The result of this attempt, however, was further persecution of Jews in all parts of Germany. Some of Jewish ancestry, and others as well, were arrested on suspicion of being connected with the plot, although there was no shred of evidence. Wittenberg was no exception. All members of Paul Bosse's family who were in Wittenberg at the time were arrested. He and his wife Kaethe, son Fritz and daughter Dolly and her husband Georg were taken into custody.

After his arrest by the Gestapo, Fritz was imprisoned for a period, and by the end of September 1944 he was taken to the work camp at Zöschen in the south of the Sachsen-Anhalt region, in which Wittenberg is situated. It was called an *Arbeitserziehungslager* – a work and education camp. It was built towards the end of the war, between August and September 1944, by prisoners from the Netherlands to accommodate hundreds of people who had been arrested in all parts of Europe, and who worked under forced labour conditions for the regime. Some 1,500 *Zwangsarbeiter* (coerced workers) were imprisoned there by the end of the war. Today Zöschen's graveyard has a monument to the 517 who died under its inhumane conditions.[4]

The reason for his imprisonment, according to Fritz, was that he was 'a half-Jew... under suspicion of taking part in the attempt to kill Hitler on 20.7.44'.[5]

Remarkably, Günther was allowed to join the army for a second time to serve as a medical officer, but in November 1944 he was dismissed, and arrested without charge and sent to a camp. The accusation made against him was that he had rejoined by stealth. It was a fortunate coincidence that he was also sent to Zöschen.

This is how he described the events in notes written after the war:

While Opa, Oma, Dolly and Fritz were arrested on 21 July 1944, it was November by the time they forced me to leave the army, as the Gestapo could only arrest members of the army directly for serious crimes. My dismissal was issued by the Gestapo's supreme command, the *OKW (Oberkommando der Wehrmacht)* with the information that no service on the front line was possible for me any longer because of the war wounds which I suffered! On 6.11.1944 I was dismissed and on 14.11 I was arrested in Wittenberg. Three days later I was taken to Halle, where completely ridiculous claims were made against me. On 30.11 I arrived at the camp at Zöschen near Merseburg, where Fritz had been since the end of September.

The prison conditions were primitive and inhuman. Fritz wrote:

> At the end of September there were between 300 and 400
> prisoners in Zöschen camp. They were all living in square Otto
> tents or in round tents (Finnenzelt). At the beginning there were
> no beds in these tents. Every prisoner would have 1 or 2 blankets
> and hay… In the Otto tents there were between 12 and 16 men,
> and in a Finnenzelt 26 men would live.

Fritz mentions the conditions and the camp's regime. During September five brick barracks containing bunk beds were built. The tents were still being used for patients and for workshops, while the kitchen and the washroom were in a wooden barracks. The watchmen stayed near the wooden barracks in the 'Roten Hirsch' – the Red Deer hotel in the village – before wooden barracks were built for them at the camp. By December there was electric light in the patients' room.

Fritz notes that men were there from many parts of Europe, including Russia, Poland, Czechoslovakia, France, the Netherlands, Flanders, Italy, some from Germany, Hungary, Denmark, Latvia, Greece, Bulgaria and two from England. Among the Russians there were many children between 11 and 16 years of age, imprisoned for stealing. Among the Poles there were some who used the trains without permission; some Czechs were there for having a relationship with German girls. Others were interred for being away from home without permission. Some Germans had been arrested for expressing anti-Nazi sentiments, and half-Jews had been accused of unknown charges by the Gestapo and for maintaining a relationship with Aryans. Two Englishmen were there for listening to radio broadcasts from England.

Many were imprisoned for a period of between eight and 16 weeks, or between twelve and 16 weeks for being in a relationship with German girls, but the authorities would often forget to release them.

The camp's overseers were SS officers. Some were members of the Party, others were Gestapo officers and most came from the vicinity. They varied a lot in nature, and some treated the prisoners violently, but others were anti-Nazi and treated the prisoners with care.

Police inspectors were responsible for administering the camp and they were responsible for clothes, equipment and money. Other members of the police also worked there.

The prisoners did not receive any mail. The warders were not allowed to say more than one word to the prisoners, and they certainly did not have permission to offer them any food.

In nearby Spergau camp, prisoners would be beaten for no reason. In Zöschen, prisoners got up at 4.45 a.m. and had to stand on their feet until 6.30 to be allocated work, often in the open air when it was freezing. From October to November, there was less standing about and fewer beatings, but a number of overseers…

would hit out in a mad rage. Bones were broken, men were made lame, and open wounds were frequent… It was clear that many of the overseers were in their element when they hit the prisoners… The overseers had pistols and rifles and they would shoot immediately if someone tried to escape.

The work of keeping order in the camp was given to prisoners who were chosen to be *Kalfaktoren* or 'minor officers'. There was a senior officer, and then officers for each nationality.

The whole camp was financed by the Leuna chemical plant, where 500 prisoners worked – and the working day was long. They caught the train at 6.19 and were back at 19.45. The railway was often damaged by bombs and they would have to walk back.

The prisoners were given a grey work suit, a pair of clogs, if some were available, but very rarely would they be given undergarments. Some men cut pieces off their blankets to make underclothes and were punished severely for this.

At midday they would have a watery soup and a thicker soup in the evening. Often the soup was made of only carrots and water. In the autumn they would have cabbage soup for a whole week, then potatoes twice a week from the middle of October. Food was rationed, and hot meals became scarcer. Bread, cheese and sausages were the main provision when available. It was not possible to sit down to eat, and food had to be eaten immediately rather than be kept, in case it was stolen. Many would steal potatoes and carrots and eat them raw.

As they were officers, of a kind, in the camp, Fritz and Günther were given various duties, but the main advantage was that they were spared the harshest treatment from the overseers. Günther wrote:

> Personally, Fritz was not treated badly by the overseers in the camp and I was rarely badly treated. Soon Fritz became the deputy administrator of the warehouse… and I took care of the patients from the earliest days. It appeared that people, because of their war experiences, had become afraid of their own bravery, it was striking how the treatment of prisoners had improved since October (that is, remarkable for the Gestapo – I hadn't witnessed people being beaten to death!). I was given the task of improving the disastrous death rate – because of famine and uncleanliness. It was a task fit for Sisyphus [6] but I was able to set about it with some success and with total commitment. While 150 of the 1,000 in my care were dying monthly, I succeeded eventually in reducing this to less than 50, in spite of receiving some from outside camps which had more frightful conditions. It is scarcely possible to describe the sights to be seen there. The most ghastly thing is how quickly a civilized man can become animal-like!

At the end of February I was officially dismissed, but I had to work 'voluntarily' as a hygiene officer – i.e. as a prisoner who could go out. I managed once to travel to Wittenberg and saw my family just before their journey to Sweden.

As Günther suggests, the hygiene conditions and health problems were atrocious. For months the camp only had one water tap. Thirty washbowls had been put in place and water was taken for these from a nearby pool. Many lost the will to keep themselves clean. It was difficult to wash and change clothes. Many arrived in the camp infested by flees, dirty and famished after spending time in other prisons beforehand. Only later, when typhus hit, did the prisoners wash regularly. Fritz said in his account:

The toilets were especially primitive. A hole, a corner in the open air, where many diseases would breed, was spreading dysentery. Later there were orderly stone toilets, but without a roof for a long time. Many of the prisoners did not bother going to the toilet, but rather relieved themselves in the night between the tents, others even in the tents, and one can hardly describe such scenes. For a long time there was no paper either. The water from the pool was dirty and it wasn't drinkable, but it was drunk as there was no coffee at all. Some of the prisoners drank pools of rain...

Prisoners who died in the camp were buried in a graveyard for foreigners, at first in wooden coffins, then in paper bags... Other prisoners would regularly take the possessions of those who died in the night, and if they had some food, they would eat it.

I witnessed how Geißler (a hygiene overseer) drove people out of the patients' barracks with a club and pistol. The patients were also staying in the Otto tents. Everyone with an infectious disease would go to the Finnenzelt, until they died. Typhus, dysentery, epidemic typhus – everyone mixed together, without beds and with only a little straw that was never changed. Healthy prisoners would take off the clothes of those who were dying and eat their food. Those who were seriously ill often used food plates as a toilet, shook the plates outside the tent and then ate again from the plates without washing them. The conditions were atrocious. I saw a German tied by his hands and feet and thrown into the tent. Although he had no trousers, he had been forced to appear each morning and stand waiting. He had been obliged to wrap a blanket around himself. The next morning he was dead. Until 30.11.44 when my brother took responsibility for the patients' barracks as a paramedic who had been imprisoned by the police, patients who could hardly get to their feet had to appear and stand for 1-2 hours...

As the prisoners had poor shoes and because they had to work in spite of their injuries, small wounds would quickly grow into big, sore abscesses.

...

Until 30.11, 6–11 men died every day. From 2.12 this decreased to 2–3 daily, as my brother succeeded in stopping the dysentery. By cleaning the two infectious tents, in order to give the patients fairly orderly accommodation, he himself caught infectious typhus and he was bedridden between 21.12 and 14.1.45. Because of his war injury his life was in danger (30.12). On 14.1.45 he started working again because while he was ill the number of patients rose from around 200 to 415.

The infections quickly spread to the overseers. As some of these fell ill, Günther was given more freedom to look after the patients. Two of the overseers died. Fritz also contracted the disease, and he had to go to the patients' barracks.

At the end of January, at the time of the typhus contagion, I had to leave the store and go to the patients' barracks. During the four weeks without a doctor, conditions had worsened. As well as working in the store I looked after my brother and also, as far as I could, those who were ill with infectious typhus, as no overseer was allowed to come to the camp and as I had survived the infectious typhus... None of them died. I was glad to be looking after the patients as I saw that I could help them. I went about it with great energy. There were enormous difficulties to be surmounted...

I had seen myself that the patients had nothing to eat for several days, and during my illness with infectious typhus I had to make an effort to keep eating. A Russian, to whom I gave my bread and food, ensured that I at least had drinking water and he heated the tent.

...

When the two wooden barracks were ready in November, the patients were moved from the tents to the second barracks. As there were no doors there, and as the oven was not giving enough heat, there was a heated argument between my brother and Schf. Reuter, who was responsible for the camp... Every morning 80-90 new ones were reported ill... As my brother had a fairly free hand at least in respect of the patients' barracks, the practice of distributing the patients was avoided. Through his regular orders enough medicine, at least comparatively, was available.

...

When I came to the patients' barracks at the end of January, I found that around 400 patients were infested with fleas, were dirty and had lost all hope; some had lost every will to be healthy. Around 60-70 of them had no clothes.

...

As the patients were moved to the new patients' barracks there was new hard work as so many were to be deloused and clothed. It was not possible to wash the patients' clothes. As far as possible, I took every free pair of pants and every free shirt for washing so that those who were new had clean clothes.

...

There would often be enough warm food, depending on who was serving in the kitchen... As far as illnesses were concerned, enteritis and kidney disorders were the biggest source of work because most people did not keep to the medical rules – such as fasting, eating food without spice – so new illnesses would still appear. Many did not report that they were ill soon enough. Others had nothing wrong with them and they reduced the care time for other patients. Most of the patients who took advantage of medical care and who showed a will to live could stay alive and get better. The ones with the least strength to resist, in spite of every

encouragement, were the Dutch, who because they had been
arrested a long time ago and were innocent, had lost their spirit.

We had to struggle against so many obstacles, which also came
from the patients themselves, that we were surprised that during
the last three months we had no more than 1 or 2 deaths a day,
almost solely due to enteritis and general weakness.

The two brothers managed to save themselves and to save the
life of scores, if not hundreds, of fellow prisoners. One of the
challenges was keeping up prisoners' morale, and then to see so
many lose spirit and become disheartened about their condition
and so lose their sense of conscience and morality:

> Some did not wash, did not keep their clothes in an orderly
> manner, they neglected their appearance and became no more than
> animals worrying about their food. They would steal the last piece
> of bread from their fellow prisoners. They would thin their soup
> and exchange it for margarine or bread, they gave cigarettes to the
> Ukrainians in exchange for clogs and then stole them back the next
> evening... Most had lost the will to help their unwell friends...
>
> By transmitting war news we received from Senders the
> Englishman, my brother and I, along with another Frenchman,
> could raise the spirits of many prisoners. If that had been
> discovered, it would certainly have resulted in death.

Towards the end of the war prisoners were released, but this
became difficult when prisoners' documents at the Spergau camp
were burnt in an air raid. Some were released every Thursday,
and sent to an employment office, but those who suffered from
infectious typhus had to stay at least another two months. The
work area was struck by bombs many times, and this added to the
time the prisoners had to stay in camp. Decisions about prisoners
were made in Berlin and many had to remain in camp for months.
Some were sent on to other prisons. The order for Fritz to be
transferred to Buchenwald did not arrive until he had spent eight
months in the prison at Zöschen.

Around 14–15 April 1945 the United States 2nd Infantry Division released around 1,000 prisoners from the labour/education camp of Spergau/Zöschen.[7] The Americans set about interviewing prisoners and cross-examining SS overseers to record the conditions in the camp and collect evidence for prosecuting those responsible for war crimes.

At the end of the war Günther and five other prisoners were ordered not to be handed over alive to the Americans. When the camp was being emptied, Fritz and Günther were supposed to have been shot. Günther noted:

> When the Americans came, the camp had to march away... and I later learned that the order was given that Fritz and I, as well as some other prisoners, were not to be taken alive by the Americans.

This order was not carried out; instead they were left alive on the roadside and rescued by American soldiers.[8]

According to Ulrich, Fritz's son, the camp was emptied and the march started to an extermination camp in the east.[9] Fritz was responsible for a horse-drawn carriage and Günther was with him. Fritz made an excuse that the horse was lame and slowly the distance between the carriage and the march grew, until eventually it was possible for the Allied forces to overtake them and ensure their release.

The United States army liberating a concentration camp

Fritz with his wife Sophie

Fritz says at the end of his memoir:

The result of the imprisonment was the same among the Germans
as among the foreigners. Hatred towards the Gestapo, hatred
towards everything Nazi. Many were shattered mentally, many lost
their self-esteem and their decency. Many became hardened.

From September 1944 to April 1945 more than 480 prisoners
died in the camp. Percentagewise the Germans and the Dutch
were hit hardest.

Ulrich wrote an account of his father's experience after the
war in the former German Democratic Republic:

After the war my father and mother married and moved to a farm
in Schatzungsstraße [Wittenberg]. From there they could supply
produce for the Bosse-Klinik as well. My father was appointed
administrator of agricultural equipment by the Soviet authorities,
because of his anti-fascist past. Clearly he performed this work
with some success as his field of responsibility increased more

and more. In time he was under increasing pressure to join the *Sozialistische Einheitspartei* [The United Socialist Party] if he wanted to continue his career. He told me that he did not want to join the *Einheitspartei*. He then set about preparing to flee with my mother to West Berlin. As the man in charge of the equipment section he could get many favours. That is how he obtained his car, for example, and he could travel to Berlin to fetch various necessities for farming.

On these journeys my father would always take personal effects (porcelain, clothes, knives and forks and pieces of his model trains and so on) to the west. Eventually he left Wittenberg with my mother and my sister and left the Soviet occupation zone illegally, settling down, after travelling through Berlin to Gehlenbeck near Lübbecke. My mother came from that area. They lived at first in a cramped space in a flat under the roof with my mother's sister. My father submitted a few applications to emigrate, including one to the United States, but he did not receive permission. He earned a living through small inventions, including agricultural equipment, and as an agricultural equipment representative. He did not want to receive compensation payments in respect of his persecution. Clearly he earned enough money through his work to be able to build a house in Lübbecke where we moved in 1953 (I had been born in the meantime). He established a company there producing small digging machines that could be mounted on tractors. The first workshop was in the garage. Later the business expanded and it moved at various times to other places. Eventually he employed around 20 people. After my father's death in 1965 the company unfortunately came to an end.

Cylch Cadwgan: the Cadwgan Literary Circle

A FTER SETTING UP HOME in Rhondda, Kate was keen to offer a hearty welcome to her husband's friends. Almost unintentionally, with her love of literature and cooking, an inquiring mind and interest in philosophy, she started a literary group. It became known as 'Cylch Cadwgan' – the Cadwgan Circle, or 'Ysgol Cadwgan' – the Cadwgan School, taking its name from their house and the mountain rising above it. Pennar Davies, the poet-theologian, Gwyn, Kate and Rhydwen Williams, the poet who returned to Rhondda as a chapel minister in Ynys-hir in 1941, became core members.

Other members of Gwyn's family, including Elizabeth Jones, his eldest sister, the first woman to obtain a first-class degree in Welsh at the University College of Wales, Cardiff; Augusta Davies his sister, and Gwilym and Dafydd (D.R.), Gwyn's brothers, also played their part. In time Gwilym became head of several schools in north Wales, while Dafydd, after periods as a minister, became a lecturer at the Baptist College in Cardiff and then at the University College of Wales, Cardiff.

Marged, Rhydwen Williams's wife; Rosemarie Wolff, who became Pennar Davies's wife; and Edna Lewis, who became Gwilym's wife, also took part. Gareth Alban Davies was a sixth-form pupil in Rhondda, and he became a keen member. Others would take part occasionally, including John Hughes the musician, the Rev. William Thomas and Sali Williams his betrothed, D. R. Thomas, T. Vaughan Lewis and George M. Ll. Davies. The latter was already a well-known minister and 'apostle of peace' – having been imprisoned during the First World War for his opposition to the conflict – he was then an MP for the University of Wales as a pacifist Christian. By this time he had moved to Maes-yr-Haf, a Quaker centre in Trealaw, Rhondda, which was set up to alleviate the suffering of workers during the coal strikes and later economic depression.

Pennar and Gwyn had both been students at the University College of Wales, Cardiff, and although Pennar had studied Welsh at school, and then at the university, it was Gwyn who encouraged him to speak Welsh. After graduating from Cardiff, Pennar went to Balliol College, Oxford and gained a B.Litt., and went from there to Yale University in America where he completed his doctorate. Their friendship continued when Pennar returned to Cardiff as a Fellow of the University of Wales, before returning to Oxford, to Mansfield College, between 1940 and 1943.

There had been no intention to formally establish Cylch Cadwgan, but Kate's hospitality played a central role. Gwyn said later:

> My wife started it by inviting special friends to stay with us at
> times, feeding them physically and spiritually. She certainly was the
> main literary spur. Nationalism and pacifism were intense creeds
> for us; also the freedom of the writer in matter and means.[10]

Exchanging ideas, discussing and challenging each other to write was the aim, while at the same time being ready to break the conventions of the day. They would read and discuss together, with Kate leading them through Goethe's *Faust* and Dante's *Inferno*.[11] Although they insisted on discussing sexual matters openly, and searched the world's religions and philosophies for inspiration, most of the members held common beliefs as Christians, nationalists and pacifists. Members of the Circle contributed a series of writings under the title *Proffwydi'r Ganrif Hon* [This Century's Prophets] in *Seren Cymru*, the Welsh Baptists' paper. Pennar wrote on D. H. Lawrence, but he and Gwyn invented, under the pseudonym of T. Griffiths-Davies, a theologian named Feodor Bashkin, from Russia, who had the idea of integrating the religions of the East and West. When he was young he had 'rebellious and immoral tendencies' but then he became 'a highly honoured visionary'. It is interesting to wonder whether this imaginary character reflected one or other of the authors.

In this series Gwyn wrote on Amenemope, Lao-Tse and Georges Sorel (under the pseudonym Nefydd Owen); Kate on Ernest Toller, Madame Curie and Lenin; Rhydwen on Mohamed; Elizabeth on George Lansbury; Augusta on Helen Keller; Pennar (under the name of Davies Aberpennar) on George Santayana and D. H. Lawrence; Rosemarie and Pennar on Zarathustra; Rosemarie on Martin Niemöller; and T. Vaughan Lewis on Mary Slessor.[12]

Gwyn was already writing under his own name and several other pseudonyms, including Nefydd Owen and Wil y Wern, to many magazines. The members wrote regularly for *Heddiw*, a literary magazine published between August 1936 and October 1942, with Aneirin Talfan Davies as editor, aided at first by Dafydd Jenkins.[13] They published around 50 poems, stories and articles (D. R. Griffiths's contributions are mainly under the name 'Lawnslod'). Gwyn published around seven poems in two other literary magazines, *Y Llenor* and *Tir Newydd* [The Litterateur and New Land].

The frivolous nature of Gwyn and Pennar is seen again in an article written by them under the name of Gruffydd Davies in *Heddiw*[14] reviewing an imaginary book by A. L. Paget-Smith, *'George Whitefield: A Study in Religious Egoism'*, where it is claimed that Hywel Harris was 'a genius drunk with the lusts of the spirit and the flesh'. One personal letter from Pennar discusses the double name of the reviewer:

> ... Gruffydd Davies sounds very natural. Dafydd Gruffydd was impossible, of course (unfortunately). [That was the Welsh form of D.R.'s name.] Would G. W. Griffiths-Davies, or something like that be too suggestive... May I see you and Käthe in 'Cadwgan' on Saturday night at seven or eight? ...

Some years later, in 1953, members of the Circle published *Cerddi Cadwgan* [Cadwgan Poems], a collection of their poems which represents their work during the war years and some other works.

The war, nevertheless, was a weighing heavily on them, as they were pacifists, and because Kate was a German of partly Jewish descent. She saw the devastation that Hitler and those who put him in power would cause. One of her poems was published in *Heddiw*, July 1940:

Cyn y storm

Mae'r cyfoethogion tewion yn gorfoleddu draw,
Yn lledu'n braf eu hwyliau i gipio'r gwynt a ddaw.
Cyn y storm.

Ar warrau'r trefwyr syber fe bwysa'r syrthni'n hir,
Lled-gofiant am hen ddyddiau, llefant am awel ir.
Cyn y storm.

Mewn ofn y gwaedda'r tlodion: "Dwg rhyfel angen in!
Ragluniaeth, Arglwydd, Führer! Rhowch gysgod rhag yr hin!
Cyn y storm!"

Fe ddaeth y storm a derfydd. Ti, fab y werin, clyw!
O cadw ac ymgeledda yr hyn a ddylai fyw
Wedi'r storm!

Before the storm

The fat rich are rejoicing yonder,
Spreading their sails finely to capture the wind on its way.
Before the storm.

On the shoulders of the sober townfolk the long drowsiness weighs,
They faintly remember the old days, the cry for a fresh breeze
Before the storm.

In fear the poor shout: "Bring us war!
Providence, Lord, Führer! Give us shelter from the elements!
Before the storm!"

The storm came and will finish. You, son of the common people, hear!
Oh keep and treasure what should live
After the storm!

Kate tried to understand the connection between the ideas of Nietzsche on the *Übermensch* (overman, or superman) and the use made of this by the Nazis. In an article in *Heddiw*, November/December 1940, she surmises that Nietzsche's claim that the common people need a dictator to instruct them would have appealed greatly to Hitler. Kate criticizes Nietzsche's failure to realise that machines were taking the place of the enslaved and that it was not possible for today's society to emulate that of ancient Greece. She also criticizes his failure to recognise the equality of women. But she also says that the Nazis had misinterpreted or completely disregarded his ideas on race. She quotes Nietzsche on the Germans, who commented that they were thoroughly mixed in race, and that they were 'more terrifying than any other nation'. He said, on the other hand, that the Jews were the 'strongest and purest race living in Europe now' and suggested that aristocratic Prussian officers would mix with the Jews. That was in complete contrast to Hitler's racism.

How would Gwyn now consider his claim at the outset of war

that he would rather side with the Germans than with the English? In August 1940, in *Heddiw*, he makes a fervent attack against Professor W. J. Gruffydd for his keen support of the war against Germany. He notes that Gruffydd sees Britain 'fighting the cause of the Catholic Church against the Extreme State'. Gwyn claims that British politicians' urge to 'secure a full bloody victory and to drive Germany to its knees' would 'inflict worse burdens than Hitlerism on the shoulders of countries'. He argues that 'Christ would reconcile his enemies rather than defeat them'. He states further that, 'by giving in to primitive beastliness a nation does not ensure the end of the old order or the beginning of a new order'.

Gwyn attacks the double standards of Germany and England in a further article in *Heddiw*, September/October 1940. With England holding on to its empire, and with Egypt still subjugated to it, he sees that England 'still enslaves India and Jamaica, although it preaches freedom for Austria and Poland; Germany will shout for freedom for India, and will give freedom to Brittany, but woe betide the Czechs and the Poles who are nearer home!'

Writing literature, as well as studying it, was a common interest to the members of Cylch Cadwgan, and the Circle took specific steps to encourage its members to do so. Gwyn also made an appeal for writers to be productive in *Heddiw*, January 1941, and it is not surprising then to find in the family papers an agreement between Pennar and Kate, and Pennar then adding a clause for Gwyn:

An agreement MADE BETWEEN

William Thomas Pennar DAVIES

and

Käthe Julia Gerthrud BOSSE-GRIFFITHS

On the thirtieth day of August 1941.

13.8.41

The agreement has two parts:-

I. W. T. Pennar Davies vows that he will in a period of not less than a year and not more than two years write a short Welsh novel of a hundred pages or more (typewritten); and that he will send to K. J. G. Bosse-Griffiths at least four pages within a month, and if he wishes, one page a week, or more. K. J. G. Bosse-Griffiths vows to prepare herself for an examination in Welsh that will take place at the same time as W. T. Pennar Davies will finish his short novel. In the written examination she will be required to

    i. Translate any part of the novel by the said W. T. P. Pennar Davies,

    ii. Translate into Welsh prose any piece of easy German prose;

II. W. T. Pennar Davies vows to write every week twenty-five words of German of his own composition and send it weekly by Tuesday morning to K. J. G. Bosse-Griffths. K. J. G. Bosse-Griffiths vows to write twenty-five words of Welsh of her own composition and send it weekly by Saturday morning to at W. T. Pennar Davies.

If these words are sent at the end of a fortnight (which will be allowed in special cases) fifty words must be sent.

APPENDIX

III. John Gwynedd Nefydd Owen Alban Lloyd Griffiths vows to write each week no less than two hundred and fifty words of any literary composition and send them each week or, if he wishes, each month to the said W. T. Pennar Davies.

The first two sections are in Gwyn's handwriting, and the last in Pennar's hand. The names following 'John Gwynedd' are ones Gwyn used as pseudonyms at various times. By learning Welsh, and becoming a part of a literary circle of this nature in Rhondda, Kate found a new life, and in the midst of the worries of war, she could close the door to some extent on her troubled past.

Rhydwen Williams, who later became a poet and novelist,

was a younger and later member of the Circle. Pennar first heard about him in 1941:

> I'm glad to hear of Rhydwen. Will you write to me soon? To give a full description of him. It's lovely to think that Ysgol Cadwgan has won a new recruit. I heard a little about him from Dafydd who was staying with me some time ago for a very short but joyful time.

The following year the personality clash between the cerebral Pennar and the flamboyant Rhydwen is felt in a note from Pennar to Gwyn and Kate, 19 January 1942:

> I saw Rhydwen in John Evans's shop last Thursday, but only for a second. I'm afraid that I took on the attitude of a stranger – in spite of myself, as it were. Our natures cannot intermingle easily outside the spell-bound atmosphere of Cadwgan. The lion and the lamb cannot lie down together...

A tension developed between Rhydwen, with his obvious talent for oral expression, and Pennar, who was more introverted and academic in nature. The two satirised each other sometime later in novels, *Adar y Gwanwyn*[15] [Birds of Spring] by Rhydwen and *Meibion Darogan*[16] [Sons of Prophesy] by Pennar.

In spite of this, Rhydwen acknowledged that Cylch Cadwgan gave a refuge of mind for those who professed pacifism in time of war. Gwyn, his brother D.R., Rhydwen and Pennar all preached, and Gwyn noted that Pennar had failed to be invited to an English church in Ammanford because he preached pacifism.[17]

Innovation and a measure of daring in literature were important for members of the Circle. Gwyn wrote to Pennar regarding an unpublished story he had sent to *Y Faner* [The Banner], the Welsh weekly news and literature paper.

Dear Bil,

A hundred thanks for your letter today. Firstly regarding *Y Faner*: we have come to a unanimous conclusion that the story's Sodomy shocked Prosser Rhys [the newspaper's editor] and nothing else. It is true that he is the author of '*Atgof*',[18] but young blood can become lukewarm with time. I read the story to Rosemarie tonight. And I'm surer than ever of its inimitable glory. This is one of the language's best stories.

The letter goes on to urge Pennar to try for a post at Caerleon College.

You know our opinion regarding this post. It has been created for you! I believe that you should certainly apply and send the necessary papers immediately. On the other hand I don't think that you should give up preaching! Strangely Merchant (although he is such a poor man compared to you) has set a convenient precedent in this direction. And I'm not sure that you should not even be ordained in time (without the care of a church). Käthe feels that you are an excellent preacher but she is doubtful whether you would fit well into the care of a church. In any case, you should not set the fact of the disappointment that Mansfield will have because of your leaving against the proper path that Providence puts before you. Think seriously about the excellent opportunity that would come to you to serve WALES! Your heart should leap at the prospect, as does my heart certainly.

Someone could think unkindly (you will argue) that you are trifling with the ministry: I say that it is your duty to preach and to spread the pacifist faith – the burning living thing that is a part of your experience – and that from Caerleon. You must remember that a preacher *who is not a minister* has an enormous advantage. From the academic standpoint Caerleon should enable you to finish your doctorate degree.

… of course, there is no certainty that you will get the job (remember the conshy-ism).

During this period Rosemarie Wolff wrote many letters to Kate. She became Pennar's wife, having been introduced to him by Gwyn and Kate at Oxford. She, like Kate, had fled from Germany because of her Jewish ancestry, and she had obtained work in the Radcliffe Infirmary, Oxford.

On 22 January 1942 Rosemary wrote (in German) to Kate after her first novella, *Anesmwyth Hoen* [Uneasy Joy] was published.

As Bil is now again in Oxford I feel that I am more connected with Wales and not so far from you.
And you know, I haven't congratulated you on your great success. That is shameful. Bil told me that you had waited for it to appear, and he was hoping to show it to me yesterday, but he hadn't come. I would like however to read it in the original text – I'm sure that you had written in German, and Gwyn had then translated. Do you now speak 'Cymraeg' well? I was quite excited when I heard… that you had won the prize and as glad as if I had won it myself…
Bil told me about Rhydwen and said that he is an 'excellent boy' – quite different from us and now I'm looking forward eagerly to get to know the character he has talked about…

The story was judged to be the best in a competition arranged by the Welsh publishing press, Llyfrau'r Dryw, and it was first published in 1941, and reprinted four times by April 1942. This was the first published volume by the authors of the Cadwgan Circle. In the book's blurb, Aneirin Talfan Davies said, 'We do not exaggerate when we say that here is an author that has jumped in one leap, as it were, to the first rank of Welsh authors.'

The novel relates the experiences of a girl coming from Wales who comes across new friends in London and Germany. She struggles with her feelings as she ventures into a new relationship. Much of the story reflects the experiences of Kate in Germany.[19]

Letters between Pennar, Gwyn and Kate about *Anesmwyth Hoen* and other literary matters show the kind of discussion that took place between members of Cylch Cadwgan. Pennar had received a letter from Aneirin Talfan Davies, who arranged the competition, and he told him (Pennar's letter to Gwyn and Kate, 3 October 1941),

Some 14 novellas came to the competition, and among them a novel from Pentre, Anesmwyth Hoen! You probably know about it. Something new in Welsh. I believe that we have here a serious new start with the Welsh novel, it seems to me to be a translation, and it's likely that Kate wrote it!

It is clear that Aneirin Talfan Davies understood the process of creating and translating, but later, when the novel was published with no suggestion that it had been translated, some reviewers criticized the Welsh. A review of the novel by J. T. Jones paid more attention to the language than to the content. Pennar said in a letter (22 February 1942), 'One can see now how utterly unfortunate was Aneirin's decision not to reveal the extent to which *Anesmwyth Hoen* was a translation from the German.'

Pennar, however, in a letter to Kate (22 January 1942) is full of admiration:

> Oh how glad I am that I am a friend of yours, and how great is the work ahead of us when we are free to do it... and Gwyn is doing excellent work with the Welsh language – the language is natural and powerful and creative, and the Welsh of the harp story is remarkably beautiful. Between everything I am full of joy and enthusiasm. The zeal which is in the story! O thank you, Käthe, thank you for ever...
>
> As a study of the adolescence of a girl, *Anesmwyth Hoen* is the best that I have read in my life.
>
> A myriad of blessings on you, Käthe, uniting Wales and literature and Ysgol Cadwgan. I'm as proud as a lord tonight. Your love and Gwyn's is the dearest and most valuable thing that I now have...

'Self-revelation' is one of Pennar's intentions as expressed in his letters to Gwyn and Kate. In a letter he wrote to both, 18 January 1942, he said, referring to daring pictures of himself that he sent to them, the context of which is his experience as a student in the United States:

I hope that Gwyn did not suffer a fatal shock when he saw 'Archangel Ruined'. He must remember that the temperature of New Haven in the summer (it was far colder than Pentre in winter) is more similar to Spain or the south of France than to Wales. The relationship between morality and temperature is worth exploring. Before long I will have to relate to you in detail the whole story of my connection with Angelo. My conscience is not completely happy when I look back. I could have been kinder to him. But it is perhaps the black cold winter that killed our relationship. But of course the episode of the Grey Lizard complicated matters...[20]

For me, eagerness is the main virtue. Lovely is the beauty of body and appearance. Sweet is the gentleness and cordiality of character. Amiable is the charm of posture and attitude, and gentility and good manners. Glorious is the sharpness and astuteness of mind. But give me eagerness. All the excellence of the gods cannot atone for lack of eagerness, for mental fear, for intellectual lethargy, for contentment of soul. Eagerness is the only thing that gives dignity to life.

In the bonds of Christ,

Pennar

You can keep the photograph. But don't show it to Mrs Rowlands!

The picture of him is an artistic one, and he added in another letter,

If this is not enough proof I must send 'Celtic Meleagros' or 'Pryderi' to you. 'Credo quia inenarrabile.'[21] But see John xx. 29...

With blessings,

Aberpennar

The title 'Archangel Ruined' is a quotation from Milton's *Paradise Lost,* and Pennar quotes two lines of the poem:

'Less than Archangel ruined, and the excess of Glory obscured'

Meleagros was a Greek hero, associated with hunting the boar. He travelled with Jason and the Argonauts in the hunt for the Golden Fleece. These two additional pictures arrived, with Pennar portraying a Celtic Meleagros in one and, in the other, pointing audaciously to the sky in his portrait of Pryderi, a prominent character in the Mabinogi, the Welsh medieval tales.

It is clear that these experiences occurred when Pennar was a student at Yale University in America. In her diary (2 April 1942) Kate notes (in German) the context of the pictures – Pennar was evidently part of the bohemian student society in that renowned university.

Other letters by Pennar mention his early religious experiences and his relationship with Rosemarie. They are a rich record of a period and of a remarkable person.

In 1942 Kate won a short story competition in the National Eisteddfod held at Cardigan. She received a letter from J. H. Lothar, the editor of *Die Zeitung*, one of the News Chronicle papers, a German-language newspaper published in London during the Second World War, asking for a German or English translation for publication, as he could not read Welsh. This story was *Y Bennod Olaf* [The Last Chapter], the diary of an 18-year-old girl who is dying, recording her feelings and emotions in an attempt to fathom the thrill of living.

The adjudicator, Kate Roberts, acknowledged as the leading short story writer in Welsh, put this story on its own in the top category, saying in her adjudication:

> We are in a completely different world by now… There is a
> great mind behind this story, a mind that can delve, through the
> imagination, into the experience of a young girl whose passions are
> starting to awaken, but whose body is paralysed. Bitter experiences
> follow this; the thoughts which stay with the dead, and eternity,
> the continuous revolt between weakness and the will to live.[22]

It is not surprising that Kate Roberts added, 'there are some unwieldy expressions in the story, the Welsh idiom is not always sound,' but she also noted, 'the style rises to high ground at times'. At the end of the story the girl hears the doctor tell her mother that there is no hope, and Kate Roberts would have preferred that the story came to an end sooner, but she adds, 'if this is a fault, it is a minor fault on a truly excellent story'.

It is possible that Kate Roberts was not keen on the condemnation of God in the last sentence, 'I have learnt how to live. I would drink the beauty of your hallowed creation with all my senses, with all my heart, with all my soul, Oh God, how can you be so cruel?'

Kate remained active creatively, and gave birth again – this time Kate and Gwyn's second child, Robert Paul, born on 27 February 1943. In time Robat Gruffudd would establish Y Lolfa publishing press, which grew into one of the most flourishing in Wales. Three years later, after the war, I was born, shortly before the family's move to Swansea. After the birth of Robert, named after his two grandfathers, Kate's diary changes to Welsh. She gives the title 'Travelling in a foreign land' to the diary with a subtitle 'The diary of Robert Paul'. The diary records her son's first months and her thoughts, but now and again she gives a taste of her life with Gwyn in Rhondda, such as the entry for 8 July 1943:

> Some argument with Gwyn regarding nurturing the baby.
> Gwyn last night in Treorchy in the open air meeting of the Blaid [the Welsh National Party] with Edna [who married Gwilym, his brother]. There was some trouble in another meeting in Ynys-hir, on Tuesday. The police came and asked for the identity cards of Gwyn and Oliver Evans for 'obstructing the road'.
> There will be another meeting in Mardy tomorrow. And Pennar will talk as well. We had a letter today. Hearty enough. The first meeting was in Ton, and the second meeting at Treherbert. Gwyn talked in Ton and Treherbert as well.

Kate wrote a pamphlet in the Welsh-language series

Heddychwyr Cymru [Welsh Pacifists], on peace movements in Germany. She received a letter of appreciation from Gwynfor Evans, written on 27 September 1943, who became leader of Plaid Cymru in 1945:

> I had an opportunity at last tonight to read your pamphlet. It is a really excellent work, and I feel very thankful for having the honour of publishing it on behalf of the Heddychwyr. It will be beneficial for the Welsh to know that there are people in Germany who have stood resolutely against war. All of your facts were new to me, and you have been remarkably diligent in your research...
>
> It would be a blessing if there were more of your type in our midst to bring Wales and the countries of the Continent nearer to each other, and so expand our horizons and deepen our sympathy with other nations.
>
> I hope you will be very happy in Bala. Some of Wales' best people live in the areas around Bala Lake.

In the autumn of 1943 Gwyn started a teaching post at Bala Grammar School, and he moved there alone initially, leaving Kate in Rhondda for a period. By now their letters are in Welsh, with the exception of one in Latin.

By 1944 both had moved to Bala, living in Manod, Arennig Street.

Kate received a request from Morris Williams, Kate Roberts's husband, who ran with her Gwasg Gee, a publishing company in Denbigh, to publish a book of short stories. Kate thanked him and Kate Roberts for praising her work. Kate published her first volume of short stories, *Fy Chwaer Efa*[23] [My Sister Eva] in 1944. The story which had won in the Eisteddfod and three other stories published in *Heddiw* magazine were included in this book.

Bala was further away from the troubles of war, and yet Kate was active in contacting German war prisoners who were kept near Bala. Within two years the war drew to a close, and Kate, with Gwyn's help, had mastered the Welsh language and had become one of Wales's most promising new literary figures. This, presumably, is what made it possible for her to keep her sanity at a time when her family was in increasing danger.

The members of Cylch Cadwgan went on to be extremely productive, although their base in Rhondda had disappeared. Gwyn wrote his first volume of verse, *Yr Efengyl Dywyll* [The Dark Gospel] in 1944, and a magazine, *Y Fflam* [The Flame] was launched with Gwyn, Pennar and Euros Bowen as editors in 1946. Euros Bowen was a poet-vicar in Llanuwchllyn, near Bala, and shared a common interest in innovative writing.

It had hardly been possible to contact Germany, and in December 1944, Kate asked Stina about the family, afraid of receiving bad news:

How are all the families in Wittenberg getting on? I must confess I fear receiving bad news about them while I am unable to see them. Give them my warmest greetings.

Kate received a reply from Stina on 18 January 1945. After thanking Kate for her letter after a period of silence, Stina says in English:

But now I'm sorry, then I have no glad news to write to you. Both your mother and Fritz are dead. Oma through bomb attack and Fritz in war. I don't know at what time. Then Edith wrote only this in November. And in her last letter was Günther very ill, so she was despaired.[24]

This was the worst possible news. But it was also incorrect. Fritz had not died and Kaethe had not died in an air raid. It is clear that reliable information was elusive during the war, even between relatives and friends. Kate found herself having to answer on 18 April 1945:

The sad news you gave me in your letter was not unexpected but has only slowly sunk in. The more I try to understand that Mutti and Fritz are dead the more they come alive to me in my memories and in my dreams. The people here have been very kind and sympathise with me. In some way it is good that my little son takes so much of my attention...

Information already given was corrected in a letter Kate received from Edith, her sister-in-law, on 13 June:

> I am with my two children for five weeks in Sweden, but I don't know where about Opa, Günther and Fritz are. Fritz is not dead, he has been in K.Z. Zöschen by Merseburg, in there Günther as sanitor laboured. After three months in Halle prison, is G. send to Zöschen as sanitor! 20 July 1944 is the family but Georg and I not sent to prison. Dolly and Opa after six weeks free. Oma is coming to Ravensbrück K.A, and there is she killed 16 Dez. 1944. The Klinik had Dr Korth. Opa is to O'T. by Osterode/Harz as Doctor. Perhaps you can hear something through Red Cross or Legation... Dolly is with four children to Dr Dolde, Wimpfen/Würtenberg. We have had a very hard time.

The letter attempts to summarise many months of suffering in the family. This time the information was correct. There were further letters from Edith during the year. One says that her husband Günther and Paul Bosse were working in a clinic in Osterode, but she did not know at the time that Günther would be allowed back to Sweden. Everything became clearer after the end of the war.

Kurt Ledien
and the White Rose

OVER THE LAST TWENTY or so years, efforts have been made in
Germany to highlight the many organisations which tried
to oppose the power of Hitler and the Nazis during the Second
World War and earlier. In the 1980s work was started to convert
the Blenderblock in Berlin into a museum commemorating
opposition to Nazism. This formerly housed army offices and
many of those connected with the attempt to kill Hitler on 20
July 1944 worked there.

Today it is the site of the *Gedenkstätte Deutscher Widerstand*,
the Memorial to the German Resistance. There is a memorial to
Stauffenberg in the yard, and the rooms of the buildings contain
exhibitions outlining around 25 different areas of resistance,
including workers' movements with the Communists, the
Socialist Workers' Party of Germany and the Social Democrats.
It has been estimated that around 350 different groups offered
resistance in Germany at various times. There is a section on the
Christians who opposed Hitler in a period when so many church
leaders bowed down in obedience. Another section tells the story
of the people who emigrated, and also relates how Jews made
attempts at resisting the system. There are two exhibition sections
of interest to the account in this book, the first dedicated to the
Weiße Rose, the White Rose movement, which operated mainly
in Munich and Hamburg, and the other detailing the contribution
of John Heartfield, one of the best known exile artists.

The Bendlerblock yard

A plaque noting where Stauffenberg and others were shot

Helmut Herzfeld: John Heartfield

On the family tree, my relationship to John Heartfield is described as 'ten times removed, through marriage'. This relationship can contain several thousand people, but one can include him as one of our family with a certain degree of confidence. A relative of his, Justus Mannchen, already mentioned when discussing Erika Viezens's story, comes to family reunions; he recently came to Wittenberg to celebrate my birthday and that of Käthe, my cousin. Although he belongs to a fairly remote part of the family, he was for a time married to Ingrid, Günther's daughter.

Helmut Herzfeld[25] was an artist and Communist by conviction. He was born in Berlin in 1891. He was disturbed by the imperialism of Germany during the First World War and decided to oppose the country's madness in a very personal way, by changing his name to John Heartfield in 1916. At the end of the war he joined the Dada Club in Berlin, a group of political and satirical artists, and he also joined the Communist Party of Germany. With others he established *Die Pleite*, a satirical

magazine, and after meeting the dramatist Bertolt Brecht in 1924, he concentrated on developing *photomontage* as a form of political expression.

When the Nazis came to power, he left Germany and moved to Prague, but with Germany threatening Czechoslovakia in 1938, he emigrated to England and settled in Hampstead. He eventually returned to East Germany after the war, and worked there with a theatre director.

Hurray, the butter is all gone,
John Heartfield, 1935

The Reich Bishop organises Christianity,
John Heartfield, 1934
(Dr Ludwig Müller, the Protestant
pastor, advocated turning the church
into a Nazi church)

And yet it moves,
John Heartfield, 1943

His powerful works satirise Germany's militarism during the first part of the century, and then Hitler especially, and the war system that offered nothing to Germany except suffering and death. It was obvious that his work would be banned in Germany during the Nazi period, and his efforts were acknowledged as a one-man battle against Hitler.

The White Rose

The Weiße Rose – the White Rose – movement has had some prominence in recent films. It started as an insignificant movement restricted to a small number of students at Munich University, with membership only possible by personal contact. It then spread to other cities in Germany, including Hamburg. Although the intention of the movement was to start a revolution that would replace Hitler, it had no more success than any other attempts. The action taken by the group of Christian students in Munich between 1942 and 1943, amounted to publishing six leaflets and distributing them, at first, in the university and then in other cities. The members were caught and executed.

A film relating these events was made in 1982, and another one, *Sophie Scholl – Die Letzten Tage* [The last days] in 2005. Brother and sister, Hans and Sophie Scholl, were central to this student movement, and so were others it seems, including Professor Kurt Huber, Willi Graf, Alexander Schmorell and Christoph Probst. The story was recorded by Inge, the sister of Hans a Sophie Scholl, in a book[26] although another member, Jürgen Wittenstein, believes their part in the movement has been exaggerated.

Sophie was only 22 years old when she was sentenced to death, her brother Hans was 25, and Christoph Probst was 24. Three others were also executed later, including Professor Kurt Huber, then almost 50, whose fields of study included psychology and philosophy.

A third wave of arrests and executions followed – among those were Kurt Ledien and four others from the Hamburg area.

Inge Scholl said that their ideas were not extreme in any way, that they did not follow any specific ideology, but simply had the aim of wishing to live humanely in a human world.[27]

The movement distributed philosophical leaflets which drew upon Germany's culture and history and the aspirations of Goethe and Schiller for the country's future and freedom. The first leaflet quotes lines of hope from Goethe's 'Des Epimenides Erwachen' [Epimenides Awakes]:

Nun begegn' ich meinen Braven,
Die sich in der Nacht versammelt,
Um zu schweigen, nicht zu schlafen,
Und das schöne Wort der Freiheit
Wird gelispelt und gestammelt,
Bis in ungewohnter Neuheit
Wir an unsrer Tempel Stufen
Wieder neu entzückt es rufen:
Freiheit! Freiheit!

I now meet my brave ones,
Who assembled at night
To be silent, not to sleep
And the beautiful word of freedom
Will be whispered and faintly pronounced
Until in an unfamiliar newness
We will on the steps of our temple
Shout it again anew with joy:
Freedom! Freedom![28]

Some of the students painted the word 'Freedom' in large three-feet high letters across the wall of Munich University and created a stir in the town.[29]

The second leaflet criticized the lies spread by the Nazis, and Hitler's book *Mein Kampf*, which they said was written in quite poor German. It also noted that 300,000 Jews had been murdered in the most barbaric manner since Germany had occupied Poland. And in the face of this and much more, according to the leaflet, the people of Germany were still foolishly silent and asleep.

These leaflets attempted to appeal to the Germans' sense of decency and took a step back in an attempt to look objectively at a Germany which had been mesmerised by Nazism and was suffering morally because of this. By not protesting against the criminal rabble, by behaving indifferently, the Germans were equally as guilty, they said.

The third leaflet called for passive resistance against the evil dictatorship. It foresaw that a victory for German fanaticism in the war would have terrifying consequences. It urged a policy of sabotage in order to obstruct the war machine.

The fourth leaflet noted Hitler's failures in the war, in Egypt and in Russia. It said, 'every word that comes from Hitler's mouth is a lie. When he says peace, he means war, and when he blasphemously uses the name of the Almighty, he means the power of evil, the fallen angel, Satan. His mouth is the foul-smelling maw of Hell, and his might is at bottom accursed. True, we must conduct a struggle agaist the National Socialist state with rational means; but whoever today still doubts the reality, the existence of demonic powers, has failed by a wide margin to understand the metaphysical background of this war.'[30]

This leaflet stated that the aim of the Weiße Rose was to restore the health of Germany's spirit, so wounded by Hitler and his regime. It was a cry of opposition against the whole structure, but it was not based on any ideology, except a belief in restoring the honour and morality of Germany.

A fifth, shorter leaflet was published in January 1943. It stated that Hitler could not win the war, only prolong it. This leaflet was not published in the name of the Weiße Rose, but on behalf of 'Widerstandsbewegung in Deutschland' – the Resistance

Movement in Germany. It asked again what action Germans were taking, and appealed for freedom of expression and freedom of belief to safeguard the individual against the might of the state's criminal power. 'In this will be the foundations of a new Europe.'[31] It foresaw that the Germany of the future would be a decentralised federal country. This leaflet was more specific in its call for Germany to rise up against Hitler, with the title, 'Aufruf an alle Deutsche!' – 'A call to all Germans!' Several thousand copies were published, and most were distributed to different towns. By February 1943 Hans and Sophie Scholl had been arrested.

The Hamburg circle associated with the White Rose had been established as a result of the first leaflet written by the Munich students. There had been a connection thereafter between the Munich and Hamburg groups through Traute Lafrenz, a medical student from Hamburg who had been studying in Munich since 1941 and had become a close friend of Hans a Sophie Scholl. In autumn 1942 she handed over the leaflets that remained after the summer of 1942 to three of the group members in Hamburg. This group listened illegally to broadcasts from Britain and met regularly in discussion evenings in two bookshops in the town.

After the death sentence was pronounced against the Munich students, a chemistry student, Hans Conrad Leipelt, distributed the sixth leaflet more widely. He lived in Vienna but had been brought up in Hamburg, and his mother was of Jewish extraction. He was thrown out of the university in Hamburg in 1941 because of his mother's ancestry, but he was accepted to the chemistry institute of Professor Heinrich Wieland in Munich, who provided places specifically to those who opposed the Nazi regime. According to Jürgen Wittenstein, Hans Leipelt was not a member of the Weiße Rose as such, and he was protected by the institute in Munich.[32] He was, nevertheless, a member of the resistance movement in Hamburg which planned to destroy a bridge with a bomb, among other things. The sixth leaflet called on students to rise up against Hitler, proclaiming, 'Germany's name will be defiled for ever unless the youth of Germany at last rises, takes revenge and rights its wrongs, destroying their torturers and builds a new, spiritual Europe.'[33]

In April 1943 Hans Leipelt and his girlfriend Marie-Luise Jahn distributed the sixth leaflet of the Weiße Rose – the last one – in Hamburg. He also collected funds for Frau Clara Huber, the widow of Professor Kurt Huber who had been hanged for opposing the system. Munich Gestapo condemned him for this, and on 8 October he was arrested. He was sentenced to death and was hanged on 19 January 1945.

Kurt Ledien was the second cousin of Kaethe Bosse, since Max Ledien, her father, was a cousin of Gertrud Levin, Kurt's mother. Although Kurt was of Jewish descent, like the rest of the family, he had been accepted into the Christian church. He was born in Berlin-Charlottenburg, the second child of Louis and Gertrud Levin. As with the family in Wittenberg, their surname was changed from Levin to Ledien in an attempt to become Germanised. The family moved to the Altona area of Hamburg, and he was educated in the *Christianeum*, an old grammar school. He fought as a soldier in the First World War and then studied law in Lausanne, Munich and Kiel and graduated in Göttingen.

He married Martha Liermann who came from Winsen an der Luhe and who kept a bookshop in Hamburg. They went to live in a flat in Gieserstraße 9, where they had two girls, Ilse and Ulla. By 1927 Kurt was a judge in a local court.

He faced difficulties like the rest of the family following the Nürenberg laws of 1933. He moved to Dortmund, but because of the ban on those of Jewish ancestry from holding public office, he was dismissed. He returned to Hamburg and found work in the legal department of Bavaria St Pauli brewery. After a while he was not allowed to stay there, and he then worked for a company of Jewish lawyers, Wilhelm Gutmann and Dr Samson, on emigration matters. While there he succeeded in arranging emigration for many Jewish families. His sister managed to reach Vienna, and his brother and family emigrated to America in 1938. However, in his own case, he did not get permission to emigrate to England until the day war was declared.

Ulla went to the *Volksschule* in Klopstockplatz and then in 1940 to the *Klosterschule* secondary school, but after an air raid that school closed, and she then went to the *Bertha-Lyzeum* in Othmarschen.[34] She had to leave that school when she was in the eighth grade because she was a *Mischling*, of mixed blood. Similarly Ilse, the eldest sister, had to leave the *Klosterschule* in 1942 and went then to a technical school and worked as a typist with an insurance company.

Kurt and his daughter Ilse were friendly with the Leipelt family, and Ilse was a personal friend of Maria, the sister of Hans Leipelt. Through Hans and his mother, Dr Katharina Leipelt, they entered the circle of the Weiße Rose in Hamburg. Kurt became a personal friend of Hans, and they discussed, among other things, what kind of Germany would exist after the fall of the Nazis. They invited others who opposed the Nazi system to their flat and,

during the war, they all met in the cellar of the bookshop at 50 Am Jungfernstieg. The group would read literature that had been banned by the Nazis and would discuss and distribute it. Students and intellectuals took part in order to express their opinions freely. After the murder of the Hans and Sophie Scholl, the group printed Weiße

The bookshop in Hamburg where members of the Weiße Rose met

Rose leaflets, distributed the leaflet 'Against Hitler and the War' and made copies of the sixth leaflet which they received through Hans Leipelt in April 1943.[35] As a result of their work, the leaflet was distributed to many countries, including Sweden, Norway, England and Switzerland. British aeroplanes dropped copies of this leaflet over parts of Germany. Because of this the group of friends became known as *Hamburger Zweig der Weißen Rose* – the Hamburg branch of the White Rose – after the Second World War.

With Jews being taken to concentration camps, Kurt Ledien

A plaque on the bookshop in Hamburg with the names of Dr Kurt Ledien and other members who died

Dr Kurt Ledien

Dr Kurt Ledien's name on the memorial in Hamburg-Niendorf

managed to save his mother, who was at the time living with him in Hohenzollerring, from being taken away. She was 76 years old and suffered from a heart condition and a bad hip. Kurt argued successfully that she would not survive the journey to the concentration camps of Poland, and he succeeded as well in the case of several other Jews.[36] But by 1943 his mother was taken to Theresienstadt, Terezín today, the concentration camp that Hitler used to deceive the authorities of foreign countries that civilized life was possible in such institutions. This camp was a kind of ghetto, and on 23 April 1945, Kurt's mother was among those who succeeded in being transferred from there to Switzerland and thereby survive the war. In exchange for 5,000,000 Swiss francs from Jewish organisations, Reichsführer SS Heinrich Himmler and other SS leaders had released 1,200 prisoners in February 1945, and by the end of April, the International Red Cross had intervened and soon took over the administration of the camp, releasing prisoners.

Between November 1943 and March 1944, 30 members of the Weiße Rose in Hamburg were arrested. Dr Katharina Leipelt committed suicide by hanging on 9 January 1944.

In September 1943 the authorities took Kurt, as well as other Jewish lawyers, to a work camp for Jews, to partake in forced labour, constructing bunkers in Berlin under the supervision of the SS. One of the other workers wrote, 'We had to do the heaviest concrete work, and moved stones and sacks of cement. Dr Ledien was not in any way suitable for the work… The work was soul-destroying.' Another one said, 'We had to work on the main security office of the Gestapo in Kurfürstenstraße building bunkers. The SS men, the *Sturmführer* and the *Obersturmführer* were supervising. The *Obersturmführer* Tuscha [Lishka, probably] had been especially harsh in mistreating and kicking many. To Dr Ledien, who had previously been a district judge and, indeed, who had not picked up a hammer in his life, the work was especially difficult. We were working together, but he was not able to work at all. But he had to. From his daughter's letters they had got to know things about him, and he was arrested. As he was ill, they took him to the police station's *Jüdischen Krankenhaus* – the Jewish Hospital. There was a department there for prisoners and those who were abducted were being watched. He arrived there eventually at the end of November 1943.'[37] It was these letters, between a father and a daughter, it seems, that gave the authorities information about his connection with the group opposing Hitler.

In the police station in Berlin his wife could provide him with clean clothes, and could receive letters from him. But on 29 February 1944 he was arrested by the Hamburg Gestapo and taken to the concentration camp at Fuhlsbüttel. Towards the end of the war the prison there had been turned into a concentration camp. The authorities had learnt about the group's meetings and the connection with the Leipelt family. Because a case for treason was being prepared, Kurt Ledien was kept in prison without a court hearing against him. A little before the end of the Second World War, 13 women and 58 men, most of them members of the Hamburg resistance cell (including some foreign prisoners), were taken from Fuhlsbüttel to Neuengamme concentration camp. The names of the 71 were put on the Gestapo's death list. Between 21 and 23 April, on the command of Graf von Bassewitz-Behr, the police chief and a leading officer of the SS, they were killed without a charge against them. Kurt Ledien was hanged in a bunker in Neuengamme on 23 April.[38]

The Gestapo had taken his daughter, Ilse Ledien, in March 1944 and had imprisoned her for treason in the Fuhlsbüttel concentration camp. She spent the first months in solitary confinement. She survived the war, as did Kurt Ledien's wife.

Katharina Leipelt
geboren 28. Mai 1893
Freitod 9. Dezember 1943

Elisabeth Lange
geboren 7. Juli 1900
Freitod 28. Januar 1944

Reinhold Meyer
geboren 18. Juli 1920
umgekommen 12. November 1944

Hans K. Leipelt
geboren 18. Juli 1921
ermordet 29. Januar 1945

Frederick Geussenhainer
geboren 24. April 1912
umgekommen April 1945

Margaretha Rothe
geboren 13. Juni 1919
umgekommen 15. April 1945

Margarethe Mrosek
geboren 25. Dezember 1902
ermordet 21. April 1945

Curt Ledien
geboren 5. Juni 1893
ermordet 23. April 1945

A plaque in the *Gedenkstätte Deutscher Widerstand* in memory of Kurt Ledien, Hans Leipelt and others from Hamburg

A sculpture in Neuengamme concentration camp

Persecuted, imprisoned and killed

THE NET THAT HAD been closing in on members of the family before the war became even more constrictive as the war continued. Kaethe, Paul's wife, as has been seen, was restricted in how much she could do in the clinic. Now she was not allowed to work there at all, and she looked after the garden which supplied food for the clinic and the family. In 1941 those working for the town administration were prohibited from using the clinic, with a threat to those that did of being sent to the front line.

Matters became more difficult for Paul Bosse. He, along with Günther, Dolly and Georg, were prohibited from using a car to visit patients. The local medical office then did its utmost to besmirch his name and that of his family. He was accused of infecting women with venereal disease, with the intention of harming the German workforce. A case was heard before the Reich's medical office on 5 August 1942, in Halle. The notes of the case state that he was married to a Jewess, and that he was not a member of the NSDAP (*Natsionalsozialistische Deutsche Arbeiterpartei* – the Nazi Party) or of the medical association of the NSD – the National Socialist Doctors' Organisation. However, the medical court judged that Paul Bosse had treated patients completely professionally.

Dolly was accused of having wrongly used deep X-ray equipment. However, she did not possess such equipment, rather shortwave rays.

Günther, Paul and another doctor had been working together on a medical book which was published in 1943 by a publishing house in Stuttgart, but this was banned by the Reich's publications' office, because of Günther's Jewish ancestry. The Reich's literature office wrote a letter on 10 May 1943 banning Günther from being an author because of his mixed blood, Category 1. The letter notes, however, that because of the wounds Günther had suffered in the war, he could make an application for special permission, but that he would have to give the details of his wounds and also information about his ancestry. This was tantamount, of course, to refusing permission once again. Without this permission, he would be punished according to paragraph 28 of the sub-sections of a law passed by the Reich's Culture Office.

The medical book dealt with using sulphonamide on bandages to treat wounds. Following the explosion in 1935 and Paul Bosse's work with patients, experience showed that it was an effective means of preventing infections. This would be especially useful in the military context. It is quite ironic that the Nazis had been willing for Günther to join the army, but had refused permission for him to publish work that could lead to alleviating wounds.

Throughout this period the Nazis attacked the reputation of the clinic and Paul Bosse. He was called a 'Jewish lout' among other things. In April 1944 an attempt was made to send his whole family away to work as gravediggers. Paul Bosse was urged to give up the clinic.

Dr Senst of Wittenberg[39] has said that the Gestapo had occupied a nearby house to watch Paul Bosse and his clinic in an attempt to gather evidence against him. Throughout the whole period, according to Dr Senst, Paul Bosse's neighbours did not betray him in any way, and the authorities had to wait until Stauffenberg's attempt to kill Hitler before arresting the whole family.

Kaethe and Paul Bosse were arrested and taken to the Gestapo police prison in Wittenberg, along with Fritz and Dolly and her

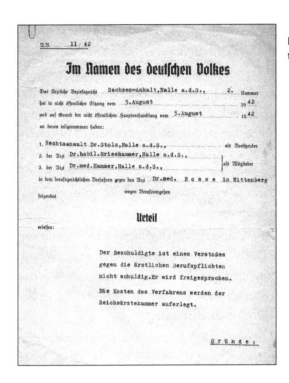

Not guilty verdict of
the medical court

The medical book written by
Paul Bosse and his son Günther
and Karl-Heinz Jaeger: *Die örtliche
Sulfonamidtherapie*. Published in
Stuttgart by Wissenschaftliche
Verlagsgesellschaft, 1943, 149pp.

223

husband Georg, or Schorsch as he was known. This was on 21 July, a day after Stauffenberg's action.

Georg was released the following day.[40] He wrote on behalf of the family to the Führer's headquarters in Berlin to argue for the release of the others. He made a special plea for his wife, as they had five children. At the beginning of September 1944, Dolly was released, having been in the Gestapo prison for six weeks without charge. On her release two conditions were laid down, the first that she should not leave Wittenberg and, secondly, that she should not operate as a doctor.

Instead she was to work on ground digging at a soap factory in Wittenberg. By now Dolly was developing a serious illness, and a Nazi doctor acknowledged this. She was released, but was not to leave Wittenberg. She was not allowed to have a maid in her home, so the maid had to be discharged.

Georg was ordered to work as a digger for the Todt organisation (the military-engineering body of the Third Reich), 'Action B'. But he was then sent to the front line as a doctor and registered as a 'B man'.

Dolly feared that the Gestapo would succeed in killing her before the end of 1944, and she fled with her family to western Germany, to Bad Wimpfen, a picturesque medieval town on the river Neckar, where she had a close friend.

Dolly and her children suffered considerably during this period of flight. The few possessions that she could take with her were carried in a pram, and they had to seek refuge in farm buildings, suffering from starvation. Her health and that of her children worsened.

Paul Bosse was kept in prison without charge for nine weeks until the end of September 1944. He was then sent to work on the aforementioned 'Action B'. He was appointed as a doctor to treat only foreigners, and without the right to write prescriptions.

He was advised by the Gestapo to divorce his wife. He refused, and because of this there were further attempts to degrade and persecute him.

According to Günther, the Gestapo officers told him, 'Because of how your mother has behaved, you will never see her again.' According to Kate, someone had told Fritz something similar.

Kaethe Bosse was, at first, kept in prison in Wittenberg. She was then moved to a prison in Halle called 'Zum Roten Ochsen', the red ox, probably towards the end of September. It is a large building not far from the town centre. From there she was moved to Leipzig and then onwards to Ravensbrück on 1 November 1944, by *Transport*, a transportation train probably. It is possible that this was a passenger train, but moving people in goods' trains was very common. By 16 December she had died. Details of her death in Ravensbrück slowly filtered through to her family.

There are two documents in existence that confirm that Kaethe Bosse was at Ravensbrück. A page documenting the *Transport* journey is one, and the other is a letter confirming her death. The first was prepared by the SS, and it notes who had been moved to the camp on 1 November 1944. Next to Kaethe's name is 'polit', short for 'politisch' – 'political'. She was not there for political reasons, of course, but because of her ancestry.

On the same page her name is given as Sara Kaethe Bosse. But Sara was not part of her name. The SS had added this to denote that she was a female prisoner of Jewish descent. The page also notes her number in prison.

Kaethe Bosse, who was in good health before her arrest, was given the number 80 911. She would have to wear a yellow triangular badge, the one given to Jews. She was there for just six weeks.

Much of the evidence in understanding what happened to Kaethe Bosse in Ravensbrück may lie in the camp conditions

The SS transport page noting Kaethe Bosse's name, no. 5 on the list

during her time there. This is available in several books published by those who had been imprisoned there, and who survived. Others have written about the prison after researching the establishment's documents.

Ravensbrück camp, one of several hundred concentration and prison camps, was around 50 miles to the north of Berlin. It was located near a railway, and a mile or so from the nearest town, Fürstenberg. The town lies on the banks of a fine lake in a naturally beautiful area, and is a centre for leisure activities. The camp's location meant that it was fairly easy to reach but also in a comparatively secluded spot.

Ravensbrück's place in the history of the Nazi concentration camps has been described as the 'hell for women'. It was the biggest camp for women in the Reich's territories. Over the six years of its existence, more than 100,000 women from more than 20 countries were imprisoned there.[41] There was also a sub-section for men and, by 1945, 20,000 men had been registered there.

Work started on building the camp in November 1938, with 500 prisoners from Sachsenhausen working there. The intention was to create a camp for 3,000 women.

One of its purposes was to uphold the Nazi military and economic system. Women worked for the textile and leather goods' factories of the SS, which were on site. It seems that between 4,000 and 5,000 women worked there daily. Other women worked for the agricultural company of the SS, and worked on the land. From August 1942 many women were forced to work in the nearby Siemens factory. By 1943 Siemens & Halske Company had built 20 work halls to promote arms production. In December 1941 between 2,000 and 3,000 women were working there. There were other arms factories in the vicinity which also profited from the free labour. Another aim of the camp commanders was to break the spirit of the women through work.

It is worth remembering that many of Germany's well-known industrial companies became rich during the war through the cheap labour of the men and women in concentration camps.

Ravensbrück was also used as a base for experimentation of various medicines. In the camp's language, the women subjected to this were 'experiment rabbits'.[42]

As stated, Kaethe was moved to Ravensbrück on 1 November 1944. That autumn Ravensbrück had been terribly overcrowded. Countess Karolina Lanckorońska made these comments on that autumn in the camp:

The blocks were now overfilled to the point where additional three-tiered bunks had to be set up in the mess halls, so that the prisoners ate and spent all of their free time on their bunks, sleeping three to a bunk. This, given the prevalence of ulcers and sores, was unspeakably disgusting...

The drainage, designed to cope with 15,000 people, was having to serve three times that number. As a result, the system was almost uninterruptedly out of order. Prisoners therefore relieved themselves in the open, near any block, as long as it was not their own. Inmates were severely punished if a passing official should take it into her head to penalise the contaminated block.

All of that was as nothing compared with what was going on in the tent. That was where, in late autumn, they put more than 4,000 women evacuated from Auschwitz (Oświecim), mostly Hungarian Jewesses. There was nowhere to breathe because there was no air; nowhere to lie down because there was no room, and nowhere to relieve oneself because the temporary latrines were unusable. Consequently, a stream of urine and excrement seeped out from under the tent, surrounding it, as it were, with a wreath of stinking puddles. Moreover, day and night there issued from the tent the ceaseless wailing and shrieking of 4,000 women, which could be heard all over the camp.[43]

This suggests that Kaethe would not have been taken to this tent, but if the huts were overcrowded and without a sewage system, it is not difficult to imagine that the squalor could have defeated her. Nevertheless, the tent was used as an admission block at exactly the time that Kaethe was taken to Ravensbrück.

Nadine Heftler said about her experience in the tent,

I was lying in the tent, without a blanket, without a straw stack, in the middle of excrement. In six days we had a piece of bread of around 250 grams only three times. In 14 days I did not have soup or coffee at all.[44]

According to SS reports, 17,300 prisoners were in the camp at the start of 1944. By the beginning of 1945, 45,637 were there.[45]

The site of the tent at Ravensbrück concentration camp

The number varies according to different authorities, as between 20,000 and 30,000 were kept in sub-camps. The total could have been as many as 65,000 by the end of 1944.

In November 1944 more than 50 transport trains reached the camp, with more than 70,000 new prisoners that month. On 1 November, the day Kaethe Bosse was transported to Ravensbrück, 1,717 women and 634 men were sent from Auschwitz to Bergen-Belsen and Ravensbrück. Of that contingent, on 3 November, 800 Hungarian Jews arrived at the camp, and 400 Polish Jews.

Jack Morrison, who researched the camp's documents, noted:

> Most of the newcomers were dumped in the blocks that had long been filled to capacity. Inmates who shared a bunk with two or three other women were now the lucky ones, as many women had to sleep on the floor...
>
> In August 1944, as the inmate population began to get out of

hand, the authorities procured a huge tent from the *Wehrmacht* [the army] and erected it in an open area between Block 24 and 26, calling it Block 25. It was to serve temporarily as the new Admissions Block, but 'temporarily' in this case was a long time, because there was no let-up in the flow of new arrivals and there were apparently no plans to build additional barracks. Because it was to be temporary, neither electricity nor plumbing was installed at first, and the only heat was that generated by the multitude of bodies huddled closely together. There were no toilets – inmates were expected to use latrines dug just outside the tent. Since it was hard to get to them at night, prisoners from other barracks sent them marmalade buckets to use as chamber pots.

Women assigned to the tent did no work. They were not permitted to leave the tent except for morning and evening roll calls, although some inmates did try to sneak into neighbouring barracks to use their washrooms. It was treated as an Admissions Block but there was no pretence at orienting the new prisoners, many of whom had previous concentration camp experience anyway...

In the meantime, conditions were so appalling in the tent, particularly once cold weather set in, that prisoners who were sick and weak had almost no chance of survival. The overseers never came inside; they were afraid to.

...

The first residents of the tent were Polish women, brought to Ravensbrück in the late summer of 1944... In October, just as the Mecklenburg weather was turning raw, a large number of Jews from the Budapest ghetto was brought it. Most of them arrived reasonably healthy, and thus their survival rate for the first few weeks was quite high... Then, in December, a huge transport of two to three thousand Jews was brought in from Auschwitz and dumped in the tent. Many did not have blankets, let alone warm clothes. If they didn't starve, they would freeze. It was at this point that the tent became, in the words of one sympathetic inmate, 'the last station on the road to death.' Those poor, starving women huddled together, lying in their own straw-soaked excrement, were condemned, and everybody knew it. The senior Russian prisoner doctor, Antonina Nikiforowa recalled, 'They died like flies. Almost the whole transport of about two thousand people died.'[46]

Whatever was the cause of Kaethe's death in Ravensbrück, it is fair to say that going to Ravensbrück was tantamount to a death sentence. After six weeks in the concentration camp, she was dead.

The family received a letter about two months later noting that Kaethe had died due to pneumonia, although the authorities, according to the note, had done their utmost to cure her from the illness.

The letter read:

Ravensbrück, 10 February 1945

Dear Dr Bosse,

Your wife, Sara Kaethe Bosse, born Ledien, presented herself 17.11.1944 as being ill and she was received to the local hospital to receive medical treatment. She was given the best care and medicine. In spite of all medical care that was given it was not possible to defeat the illness.

I offer to you my sympathy for this loss. Your wife had not expressed any last wish.

I have instructed the prisoners' possessions office of my camp to send her possessions to those with a right to receive inheritance.

[signature of the section leader of the SS]

Later, Kaethe's ashes were sent to the family home. But, could one believe that these were the ashes of Kaethe, any more than one could put credence to this letter?

It was realised in time that the letter was remarkably similar to letters sent to thousands of other families in all parts of Germany regarding those who had died in various concentration camps. The text, therefore, was composed centrally and used by many concentration camps. It was realised then, if not earlier, that there was no truth in its message.

Ravensbrück, den 10. Februar 1945.

Sehr geehrter Herr B o s s e !

Ihre Frau, Sara Käthe B o s s e geb. Ledin, meldete
sich am 17.11.1944 krank und wurde daraufhin unter Aufnahme im hiesigen Krankenbau in ärztliche Behandlung genommen. Es wurde ihr die bestmöglichste medikamentöse
und pflegerische Behandlung zuteil. Trotz aller ange-
wandten ärztlichen Bemühungen gelang es nicht, der Krankheit Herr zu werden.

Ich spreche Ihnen zu diesem Verlust mein Beileid aus.
Ihre Frau hat keinen letzten Wunsch geäußert.

Ich habe die Gefangeneneigentumsverwaltung meines Lager
angewiesen, den Nachlass an den erbberechtigten Empfän-
ger zu senden.

SS-Sturmbannführer

The letter from
Ravensbrück
informing of
Kaethe's death

Dokumente aus dem Dritten Reich

Herrn Albert Reichert,
Stuttgart-Gablenberg,   Dachau 3/V, 26. 11. 42.
Hauptstr. 111.

Sehr geehrter Herr Reichert!

Ihr Vater Albert Reichert, geb. 11. 3. 76, zu Stuttgart, meldete sich am 6. 11. 42 krank und wurde
daraufhin unter Aufnahme im Krankenhaus in ärztliche Behandlung genommen. Es wurde ihm die best-
mögliche medikamentöse und pflegerische Behandlung zuteil.

Trotz ärztlicher Bemühungen gelang es nicht, der
Krankheit Herr zu werden.

Ich spreche Ihnen zu diesem Verlust mein Beileid aus.
Ihr Vater hat keine letzten Wünsche geäußert.

Die Zusendung des Nachlasses wird mit der Staats-
polizeileitstelle Stuttgart geregelt. Sie erhalten Be-
scheid.   (gez.) Weiß,
                        SS-Sturmbannführer

A similar letter
sent to families
throughout
Germany

In a similar letter published in a newspaper, it was seen that the general wording was exactly the same, but that dates of birth, illness and relationship had been changed.

Months later, Paul received a letter from a woman whose husband had been in prison with his son Fritz. It seems there was a general ignorance regarding prisoners. The letter addresses Kaethe Bosse, and the author, Emmy Schlegel, clearly did not know of Kaethe's fate.

16.9.1945 –

Dear Frau Dr Bosse,

At last I have an opportunity to write a few lines. I hope that you, like me, are back with your dear relations. We have in common many difficult hours behind us. Is your son Fritz also home? I saw him last in Zöschen, near Leipzig. He was with my husband. I gave both regularly an extra portion of food. I haven't heard from my husband since the beginning of December, perhaps your Fritz can give you some information about my husband. He *should* be released at the start of December. Perhaps he has become a soldier. So I wonder could he remember? My husband was working in the horses' stable, and I was in the kitchen and food barracks (bread, butter, sausage). We [the carer Marta and Emmy] often brought food for Fritz, who was in the clothes room. If he is there, I will send a picture of us.

...

A thousand greetings,
Emmy Schlegel
Neutz,
Halle

A year passed by before Paul received a letter from Frau Salzmann, from Großtreben, not far from Wittenberg. This was quite a surprise, although Paul had made many attempts to get to know the circumstances of his wife's death.

Großtreben, 5.7.1946

Dear Herr Bosse,

As I learnt today that you are at home, allow me to write a few lines.

I was myself with your wife in Halle and in Ravensbrück. She always asked me if I could visit you but I was not released until July last year and as I had been seriously ill it was not possible for me to travel. The fact that your dear wife will not come back again causes me great pain. She always said that she would not survive. It was really terrible. They had caused her too much pain. If I can I shall call on you in the near future if that is all right with you. I will then tell you how it was with your wife. Please answer.

Greetings, Fr. Salzmann

In a letter which he wrote to his daughter Kate on 1 August, Paul noted a part of the conversation which he had with Frau Salzmann. She told him:

I am a mother of 6 children. My eldest daughter is 17 years old. My husband is still in prison. In April 1944 I was arrested, because I had transferred letters to foreign people. I came to Halle and there I met your wife at the end of July. She made an impression on me through her unassuming and withdrawn manner and her attempt to keep herself and her clothes clean all the time. As I was a caretaker, I had quite a bit of comparative freedom, I could see in your wife's file that she had been taken into custody only because she was a half-Jewess and that she had to go to a camp... [This probably refers to Paul Bosse's discovery of a French admiral Aryan among her forefathers.]

I had to inspect your wife for head lice and I was supposed to cut her hair off. I refused to do this. And as our cell for 30 women had been overfilled, I had permission to choose two women with whom I could share a smaller cell. I had permission to take your wife with me. Here things were comparatively good for us, as the cell was never closed and I, as caretaker, could go in and out continuously. I could also give your wife various things. Your wife was given the task of repairing things, but she sometimes had to deal with filth. We could only wash and change clothes every few weeks. Once again I smuggled a letter from your wife. But because she had written the name of the sender on it, the letter came back. [It seems that one letter written by Kaethe had reached Wittenberg, and was sent on to Knubben, but Frau Salzmann was not aware of this letter.]

Frau Bosse had always asked for a cross-examination, [presumably so that she could try to convince the authorities of her contribution and that of her family to medical affairs in Wittenberg] but every time she was sent back with the words, 'We have better things to do than worry about such unimportant matters.'

When I told her eventually that we were to go to a camp, she wept bitterly. She was afraid that we would be transported to Auschwitz…

As Paul investigated further, he received a letter from Erika Buchmann, of Stuttgart, dated 9 March 1946. She had been working in the patients' section at Ravensbrück. She said:

I'm sorry that I have no news to give you about your dear wife. You know how overcrowded our camp was and how little individual prisoners knew of each other. I myself was working in the section for patients, but I was in the part that dealt with lung illnesses, and not in the main section. I can say quite definitely that your wife did not suffer from tuberculosis – I have not forgotten the names of any of my friends from that block…

I have the impression, based on your comments, that you have received a note from the camp administration that let you know about the death of your dear wife. If so it must note the cause of her death. A diagnosis of 'heart weakness' could be true – because during these weeks and months thousands of our friends died of this. As you want to know the truth, I must tell you that most women were short of food, so that most of them suffered from typhus, and so one could with some truth say that they also suffered from weakness of the heart, because in most cases the heart of those suffering from this illness could not withstand it.

Spare yourself, and your children, and me likewise, from a detailed description of our living and our dying in Ravensbrück... But take one comfort: friendship in the camp was very great, especially among the political prisoners, and the likelihood that your wife did not die on her own must help you...

May I finish, respectful Doctor, by saying that we who have survived the war and the camp now live in memory of our dead. We have taken the responsibility of their prayers when dying for the battle to ensure that concentration camps and Nazism and war will never again be seen in Germany.

We will no longer know the truth. It is possible that Kaethe had a fatal illness in the tent or in the barracks. It is possible that she was punished by the camp overseers. There remains another possibility, the gas chambers. In the last period of the camp, the SS destroyed much of the evidence that could prove they behaved in an inhuman way. There is evidence, nevertheless, that a gas chamber had been built in Ravensbrück. Women would be told that they were being sent to another camp named Mittwerda.

Ravensbrück concentration camp

But Mittwerda did not exist. It is likely that these were sent to a gas chamber built near the crematorium, a little beyond the camp walls. A list exists of 480 women who were sent to Mittwerda, including those of Jewish, Sinti and Roma or 'gypsy' descent.

The SS officer Schwarzhuber said:

> There were always 150 women who were forced into the gas chamber at one time. *Hauptscharführer* Moll ordered the women to undress and told them that they were going to be deloused. They were thereupon sent into the gassing room and the door was closed. A male inmate, wearing a gas mask, climbed onto the roof and threw a canister into an opening, which he immediately closed again. I heard moaning and whimpering from inside. I can't really say whether the women were dead or unconscious because I was not present when the room was cleared out.[47]

Tins of Zyklon-B were found in the camp after it was liberated. Some of the prisoners remember smelling the sweet gas, and suffered from headaches:

> One day we went into the barracks which was just a few metres from the crematorium to fetch washing powder for the laundry… The room was filled with a sweet smell, after which we had a nasty headache. There is no doubt: here, in the second half of the nondescript barracks, was the awful chamber, where hundreds of people were killed daily.[48]

Any further research would be in vain.

This information was slow to reach Wales. Kate had not seen her parents since before the war, and corresponding had been especially difficult during that time, with letters and occasional telegrams exchanged through the Red Cross.

On 31 January 1945 Paul wrote to his daughter in Wales, in a note restricted to 25 words:

My dearest Kathrinchen, Letter of April received. Oma died on 16.12. Warmest greetings to the three of you from Knubben, Ingrid, Stina, Dolly and her 5 children,

    Your father,

    Paul Bosse

The letter to Paul giving information regarding the death of his wife was written on 10 February. The note written by Paul states 31.1.45, so it is probable that he had heard of his wife's death earlier. Kate's answer is on 30 April, so presumably there must have been delay in delivery:

It is difficult to believe that I will not see our dear mother or Fritz ever again. Is Günter still alive? Full of longing,

    Your three [Kate and Gwyn and their son Robert],

    Kate Griffiths

In his note, Paul had named some members of the family, including Knubben (Günther's wife), Ingrid and Stina (the daughters of Günther and Knubben) and Dolly (Kate's sister) and her five children. There is no mention of Fritz, and Kate takes for granted then that Fritz was dead.

By January 1942, 1,400 men and women, most of them of Jewish descent, had been taken to be killed in the Bernburg gas chamber near Magdeburg. During the following months prisoners were transported to be killed in other camps including Majdanek and Auschwitz.

Ravensbrück, then, was playing its part in the extensive programme of exterminating Jews. It has been estimated that 60 transporting journeys were made to Ravensbrück, with between 60 and 1,000 prisoners on each journey.

During the final months at the prison, the lack of hygiene was serious and typhus had taken hold. In January 1945, 45,070 women and 7,848 men were there, and the overcrowding was appalling. On 3 April 1945, 300 women from France were

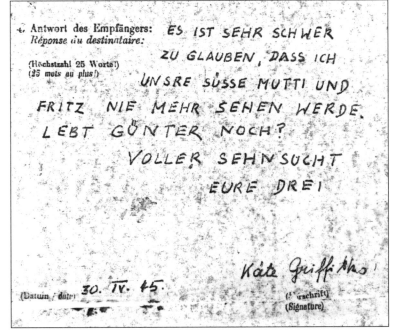

npfänger .. ..Käte Griffiths.. .. ..
estinataire
.. ...Cadwgan,14 St.Stephen Avenue.. .. ..
Pentre 6Rhondda) S.Wales
.. ..
folgendes zu übermitteln Great Britain:
ce qui suit:
tzahl 25 Worte!)   Liebstes Kathrinchen,April Brief
ts au plus!)   erhalten.Oma am 16.12. gestorben.Euch drei
herzlichste Grüsse von Knubben Ingrid Stine
Dolli und ihren 5Kindern
Dein Vater.

tum / date)   31.1.45.   (Unterschrift / Signature)
pfänger antwortet umseitig

A note by Paul Bosse on his wife's death

.. Antwort des Empfängers: ES IST SEHR SCHWER
Réponse du destinataire:
ZU GLAUBEN, DASS ICH
(Höchstzahl 25 Worte!)
(25 mots au plus!)   UNSRE SÜSSE MUTTI UND
FRITZ NIE MEHR SEHEN WERDE.
LEBT GÜNTER NOCH?
VOLLER SEHNSUCHT
EURE DREI

Käte Griffiths

(Datum / date) 30. IV. 45.   (Unterschrift)
                                       (Signature)

Kate's note to her father believing that her mother and her brother Fritz were dead allowed to go to Switzerland under the care of the International Red Cross. On 8 April women from Scandinavia were released and started their journey to Neuengamme. (In another chapter we have seen that Kurt Ledien had been killed there.) On 22 April, a further several hundred Swedish women were released, and the last goods' train, with 3,960 women, mainly from Poland, travelled in the direction of Denmark and Sweden on 26 April – 7,500 women were released in this manner.

Of those who were left, 20,000 started a death march towards the West. After their departure on 29 April, and after the electricity and the water had been turned off, 2,000 detainees were left in the prison. On 30 April the front-line troops of the Red Army arrived near the camp, and the camp was freed. A deputy sergeant of the Red Army described what he heard and saw:

> The Russians have come! The news spread like lightning through the camp. On all sides women came running to us, wiping tears of joy from their eyes, which flowed spontaneously. Hundreds of women, each one thin, ill, in dirty striped clothes. Everywhere thin hands were stretched towards me. In all languages words of greeting and thanks flowed. I could not understand them. I was disturbed and shaken by what I saw.[49]

PART 4

AFTER THE WAR

Paul Bosse

U PON HIS RELEASE FROM prison in 1944, Paul Bosse was sent by the Gestapo to Osterode, a small delightful town of some 25,000 people in the Harz mountains. After consultation with the authorities he worked as a gynaecologist and then spent some time there as a general practitioner after the war. He was, however, suffering from illness, and Günther took over his work, allowing him to go to Dolly's home in Bad Wimpfen for some time before taking up work again as a doctor in Wittenberg.

Paul's diary of this period suggests that things were hard. On 25 November 1945 he wrote how much he was missing Kaethe:

> No home, no-one to care for me, no-one wants me. Everyone
> is busy with their own worries, and some greater ones, so
> they cannot take the additional burden of me. I must try to be
> independent once again and trust in the help of strangers for my
> pay, until the bitter end.

In a letter to Kate from Bad Wimpfen, he wrote:

> Everything has been frozen solid here for some time. I hope
> we can continue through everything. Dolly had some wood
> yesterday. I don't know how long it will last. Günther has coal
> and that lasts longer. You are quite right. I must go back to
> Wittenberg, and on 16.12 your mother will already have been
> dead for a year. I have made every effort to be in Wittenberg on
> that day but unfortunately I haven't had permission to travel...
> And in this weather I cannot travel. The strain would be too
> much for me.
> Just as I'm finishing this letter, a messenger from Wittenberg

comes with a letter from the Oberbürgermeister that Paul-Gerhardt-Stift wants to accept me back. I will travel there on 13.12…

On 6 December the office of the Mayor of Wittenberg released a notice calling for the return of Paul Bosse to Wittenberg and for every assistance and protection to be given to him once he was back. It noted that the population of Wittenberg was increasing rapidly as people were moving from the East, and it wished that Paul Bosse be restored to his former post as senior doctor at the Paul-Gerhardt-Stift.

The offer was not quite so generous, however. In his diary, which contains details of the complicated arrangements of the hospital and clinic, Paul says that the Paul-Gerhardt-Stift offered him the post of senior doctor – but only in a sub-section of the hospital at 26 Heubnerstraße, his own home. Paul says:

… that is what I call strange pastoral cheek – the senior doctor of my own clinic, through the grace of P.G.St. Then they offered me the birth section of P.G.St… I know why I want to remain free.[1]

The hospital had occupied the clinic and taken its possessions during his absence, and he had to struggle to recover whatever he could. Paul remarked:

… P.G.St. had left the clinic in a pickle during the hard days, with all the doors open, with no-one there, so that the place was free to be ransacked.

A little hope for the future came as Christmas approached, with relatives and neighbours coming together to celebrate the occasion in each other's company. On one occasion Paul asked everyone to tell stories relating to their wedding.

The clinic, after the disruption, had been left empty, and had in the interim been used to provide accommodation for foreigners. A complete refurbishment was needed, starting from nothing. On 31 December 1945 Paul wrote to his children to say that he

Abschrift!

Der Oberbürgermeister
der Lutherstadt Wittenberg
Fernruf 3251

Dienststelle: - Wohlfahrtsamt -
Betreuungsstelle
"Opfer des Faschismus"

6. Dezember 1945.

Reisebescheinigung

Herr Hans L o s s o , Elektriker, geb. am 16.5.28 in
Limbach, wohnhaft in Wittenberg, Bismarkstr., ist beauftragt
Herrn Dr. med. B o s s e , geb. am 8.3.81, von Bad Wimpfen
Neckar nach Wittenberg zu holen. Selbiger beabsichtigt,
seine Tätigkeit als Arzt wieder aufzunehmen, da er in
Wittenberg dringend erforderlich ist. Obiger wurde auf
Grund der Vorgänge vom 20. Juli 1944 und seine Frau Jüdin
war, andauernd verfolgt und am 21. 7. 44 mit Frau und
Kindern verhaftet. Seine Frau Käthe Bosse ist im KZ.Lager
Ravensbrück am 16. 12. 44 auf Grund von Mißhandlungen
verstorben.
Ich bitte alle Behörden und Verwaltungen, ihn auf seiner
Fahrt nach Wittenberg Schutz und Hilfe zu gewähren. Die
Stadt Wittenberg hat grösseren Bevölkerungszuwachs durch
die Ostumsiedler und es ist erwünscht, dass Dr. Bosse in
seine alte Stellung als Chefarzt im Paul Gerhardt-Stift
wieder eingesetzt wird.

Der Oberbürgermeister
- Wohlfahrtsamt -
I. V. gez. Unterschrift
(unleserlich)

Sachbearbeiter:
gez. Albrecht

Opfer des Faschismus
Betreuungsstelle Stadtwohlfahrtsamt
Lutherstadt Wittenberg

Vorstehende Abschrift stimmt mit der Urschrift überein,
was hiermit bescheinigt.

Bad Wimpfen, den 10. Dezember 1945.

Der Bürgermeister.
J.A.

The letter from the Oberbürgermeister recalling Paul Bosse

had taken possession of the clinic, that he was the senior doctor of a similar department in the Paul-Gerhardt-Stift and that he was able to conduct operations there with the sisters. He was also the senior doctor of the hospital for war returnees, with more than 450 beds. During that year he wrote long letters to Kate and his other children, obviously heartbroken at the loss of his wife, but also full of plans for the future.

On 6 April 1946, exactly ten years after establishing the partnership with the *Marienschwestern,* the first mother arrived to give birth at the clinic. The number of patients increased quickly, and Paul Bosse started holding surgeries there.

However Dr Jonas, his successor at the clinic, said that Paul was by now a broken man. On 15 December 1946, he suffered a heart attack. He was living at the time in Schatzungsstraße with his son Fritz, and this same house was Günther's address as well, although Günther still occupied 14 Lutherstraße. He called on Dr Jonas to visit him, and asked him to lead the clinic in his place. He lived for another three months after this, and died on 5 March 1947. Dr Jonas said, 'He was an excellent surgeon and obstetrician, a sure and swift operator, and mainly a kind and likeable man.'

The funeral service was held at the clinic. Many relatives and friends attended. An address in his honour was given by Dr Wachs, who had been a colleague of his and in charge at the Paul-Gerhardt-Stift.

His son Günther could not take over the clinic because he had not finished his studies as a gynaecologist, but he would come often from Osterode to Wittenberg to help with treatments. The gynaecological workload there was heavy at the time, and operations would take place on two days a week. After a short while, Günther moved to Sweden and became a doctor there.

Dr Jonas was the only maternity unit doctor in Wittenberg at the time; he had studied in the women's department of Leipzig

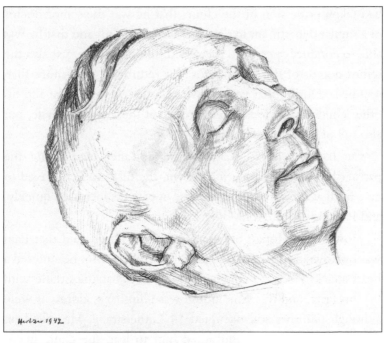

A sketch of Paul Bosse's
death mask, 1947

The family grave in
Wittenberg

University and had worked in Wittenberg since 1936, but had spent the war as a doctor for a mobile military unit, including maintaining a hospital on Russian front from 1941 to 1945. Dr Jonas led the clinic until 1973.

Care for the clinic changed from the *Marienschwestern* to *Caritasverband*, a Catholic establishment, with Dr Jones at the helm. Dr Erhard Sauer came to the hospital in 1970 and took over from Dr Jonas, an arrangement that lasted until Germany's reunification in 1989.

This event meant that families who had lost their homes had a right to be given compensation. Kate refused her compensation on condition that the name 'Bosse' remained on the clinic. Following financial difficulties, the hospital was transferred to the *Alexanierbrüder*, an old Christian order founded in the 15th century. A psychiatric department for Klinik Bosse was established in Puschkinstraße 7, a building in the *Jugendstil* style, and the use of the clinic in Heubnerstraße for births came to an end in June 1996. With the old buildings needing considerable attention, and medical advances calling for new standards, a start on building a new hospital was made in September 1997 in Hans-Lufft-Straße. This was opened in April 1999 and still uses the name Bosse.

In 2009, a small commemorative plaque was placed in the pavement in front of the original clinic in Heubnerstraße in Wittenberg, noting the fate of Kaethe Bosse.

Nona and her children, Greta and Gwenllian, in front of the new Klinik Bosse, 2010

A plaque in memory of Kaethe Bosse in Wittenberg

Dolly

DOLLY, KATE'S SISTER, FACED a disturbing future following her arrest. She was released after being imprisoned for five weeks, following Georg's appeal to the Nazis, although there is no certainty whether it was his appeal that secured her freedom. Her small son, Peter, had already died after an accident with a knife when the family was out on a picnic.

Dolly had a difficult personal life during the war. She was not able to marry her first and great love, so married Georg, who was a teacher. He was dismissed from his job because of the marriage to Dolly, but went to Freiburg to study dentistry. Georg was the name given to their first son, who later gave himself the name Tippen, which he was known by throughout his life. He developed diabetes as a young child. Although he led a full life – he became a doctor, married and had a son, Juri, who lives in Berlin – the illness caused him to lose his sight. He then suffered from kidney failure, and died at the young age of 37. Paul Bosse idolized Tippen, and became a second father to him.

The relationship between Paul Bosse and Georg was difficult. It seems that Paul could be critical of him, maybe because he did not possess his energy and drive. It is possible that this could have been the cause of Dolly's illness – said by Günther to be possibly psychosomatic – but the illness was nevertheless quite serious. Georg and Dolly had three children, the two boys and a daughter, Barbara.

The relationship between Dolly and Georg was strained in the war years, and the rift between them became apparent. Later on, there was evidence that Georg was involved with someone else in Wittenberg.

During this difficult period Dolly rekindled her relationship with her first love, and before the end of the war they'd had three children, Ecke, Roswitha and Ute, the second of whom was brought up by him. This was the background of Kate's novel, *Mae'r Galon wrth y Llyw* [The Heart is at the Helm] published in 1957, in which she discusses the tension between the search for love and society's moral presumptions.

When the war came to an end, the Russians reached Wittenberg and, as is common in war, their behaviour was vicious. All inhabitants were prohibited from leaving the town, but Dolly fled westwards with three of her children. At one time they passed a column of marching refugees, and a bomber plane flew so low that they could see the pilot's eyes. He shot indiscriminately at them.[2]

Dolly's aim was to reach either Baden-Baden or Bad Wimpfen, on the banks of the Neckar, some 50 miles from Heidelberg. Bad Wimpfen is a town of *Fachwerk* (timber-framed) houses with two churches, on a hill within old town walls. There, in a house on a flat piece of land not far from the river and under the shadow of the town wall, was the home of her lover, who was the head of a salt factory. Dolly then lived in a house at the far end of the town, a little outside the old town's walls. Georg, Dolly's husband, joined her in Bad Wimpfen.

Dolly described some of this in a letter dated 2 December 1945 to Kate, from Bad Wimpfen:

> Receiving your first letter after 6 years was a stirring experience... You can hardly imagine, in spite of all knowledge, how much the world has changed for us. None of us is the same person we were six years ago. We live in a world that has been utterly transformed, a world of continuous uncertainty, a world where we struggle again to build a future, but without being able to trust in one day.

Dolly, from her later period in
Baden-Baden

Bad Wimpfen

I ran away at the end of March with three children (Tippen was with Opa in Osterode, Roswitha with the Doldes in Wimpfen) in Wittenberg from the Gestapo and the Russians with Baden-Baden as our aim. But we did not reach Bavaria, as the war had come too close to us. There on Easter Sunday, in an open field, there was a huge attack that lasted twenty minutes – with three children, it was horrible. With the tanks moving nearer and nearer, with air attacks more fierce all the time, we experienced the end of the war, which came – after I fled to a place for treating patients for the third and last time – quite peacefully. I went on a journey of 150 kilometres, with the pram and the children, as far as Wimpfen. Our plans for Baden-Baden had come to nothing for the time being and so we stayed in Wimpfen.

We are now living in a small, pleasant house but almost without furniture in a lovely country among half-mad people. Opa lives with Tippen in the home of the Doldes. We, and Opa mainly, are struggling with the idea of going back to Wittenberg, where everything would be much simpler and economically sounder but unfortunately the Russians are there.

The first memory of Barbara, Dolly's eldest daughter, who was seven years old – she cannot remember anything earlier than that – is of the American soldiers who had occupied Bad Wimpfen ordering a curfew, with no-one allowed out of their home. Without hearing, or without understanding, or without obeying, Dolde's mother-in-law stood on the street, and Barbara saw her being shot dead.

For Ute, Dolly's second daughter, however, the ten years she spent in Bad Wimpfen were paradise.

Already in the 1920s, Paul had bought a house in Baden-Baden in the north of the *Schwarzwald* – the Black Forest – intending at one time to give it to Kate. The house was occupied by French soldiers for a period after the war, but when it became available, Georg and Dolly moved there, and Dolly set up a surgery and a flat of her own in nearby Salbach.

Dolly worked as a doctor throughout her long life. Her children, Tippen, Barbara, Ecke and Ute became doctors, specialising in various medical fields.

She died on 3 July 1993.

Günther

BEFORE THE WAR GÜNTHER had been called up for military service in the period between March and May 1938. Then, at the outbreak of war, he was called up to the army, with Flak. Regt. 43, and served as a medical officer. As already noted, he suffered serious chest injuries and was therefore released in 1940 and worked in the family clinic until 1942. He was recalled to army service in November 1942 and in 1943 worked as an assistant doctor in Eilenburg, and then from 1 November 1943 to 6 November 1944 in a hospital for soldiers in Eisleben as a surgical assistant, treating soldiers who had been badly injured. Later he received a reference from Dr H. Harttung, the chief doctor there, praising his work (16 June 1945).

In November 1944, as already mentioned, he was dismissed from the army by the Gestapo and sent to Zöschen prison camp on 30 November 1944. He spent several months there as a 'sanitary officer' and he was there until he was freed in May 1945. He stayed in Zöschen under the new American administration for a short while.

When it became possible to leave Zöschen, Günther tried to find his father in Osterode, and decided to stay there serving the new administration. In December 1945 he was appointed adviser to the military government of the Osterode region.

It was now possible to contact members of the family who had gone to Bad Wimpfen, and on 18 October 1945 Günther received a letter asking him to visit them before the end of the month with a supply of plaster, as there was a great shortage.

Günther's citizenship
document, 1937

Günther's wartime
disability pass

From March 1946 Günther worked in Osterode's town hospital as a surgical assistant and in the gynaecological department, but he still found it difficult to be recognised by the authorities as a gynaecological doctor as he did not have sufficient experience following his studies. Since the status of doctor was refused to him under the Nazi system, the new authorities could not recognise the period he had been working in his father's clinic or the period of general work in the army and in the camp. They insisted that he should have experience of two bigger hospitals (letters: 13 August 1945 and 19 November 1945). This meant that he could not take responsibility for the Klinik Bosse in Wittenberg. He stayed at Osterode until 1948.

Günther then decided to go to Sweden, and there he established a surgery in Karlshamn, on the south coast. He learnt Swedish and raised four children, Ingrid, Christina, Ingegerd and Polle. He became a well-known local doctor, and with his interest in sports he became doctor to the local football team. He visited Swansea many times, and his favourite view in the world was seeing Rhossili Bay from the cliff top. During one visit he sensed that he would not see that view again and, a year or two later, knowing that he did not have long to live, he asked me to visit him in Karlshamn – better to go there when he was alive than to be present at his funeral, he said. That is when he related to me, in long conversations, some of his story, and he wished his story to be recorded.

He emphasised the remarkable strength of the family members who survived the war, which made it possible for them to live creatively and positively, although they had a bitter taste of the most evil regime of the western world, a world so often and so wrongly regarded as civilized.

A page of a Halle Gestapo document giving Günther a role at Zöschen as a health officer. It says that he must act in complete secrecy or be prosecuted, 23 February 1945. He normally worked a 70-hour week.

Günther's residential certificate at Zöschen, prohibiting him from leaving the town, 22 May 1945

Military Government - Germany
(Militärregierung - Deutschland)

LETTER OF APPOINTMENT OF COUNCILLOR
(Ernennung zum ~~Gemeindevertreter~~/Ratsherrn)

To   Herr Günther Bosse
(an)

of   OSTERODE
(wohnhaft in)

1. Having been suggested your name in dealing with the formation of the Representative Council of Kreis Osterode, after consultation with the Landrat of this Kreis you are hereby appointed Councillor of the Kreistag

   (Für die Bildung des Kreistages Osterode ist Ihr Name in Vorschlag gebracht worden und, nachdem der Herr Landrat darüber befragt worden ist, werden Sie hiermit zum Ratsherrn für den Kreistag ernannt.)

2. It is expected that your activity as a member of that Council will contribute to the efficiency and smooth running of the Administration of this Kreis to the benefit of all its inhabitants.

   (Es wird der Erwartung Ausdruck gegeben, daß Sie in Ihrer Eigenschaft als Mitglied des Kreistages dazu beitragen werden, die Verwaltung des Kreises tatkräftig und reibungslos zum Wohle aller Einwohner zu gestalten.)

11 Dec 45

Osterode/Harz

(F. G. CORIN)
Lt. Col. S. O. I
Comd 608 (K) Det. Mil. Gov.

A letter appointing Günther on the council of Osterode

Günther and Lotte, his second wife, at Rhossily for the last time, 1995

Fritz

FRITZ HAD BEEN A keen member of the *Pfadfinder* – a movement similar to the Scouts – at the beginning of the 1930s, and when the war came he joined the army and served in Poland. He was dismissed in March 1940 and allocated land work, and then, as we have seen, he was arrested with the rest of the family by the Gestapo.

Fritz wrote a letter to Kate on 1 November 1945 noting concisely what had happened to members of the family towards the end of the war. By then he added that he and his wife were the only family members left in Wittenberg. He said in a later letter, on 27 January 1946, that he had found his sweetheart Sophie after he had been released from prison, and they married on 20 May 1945, and returned to Wittenberg. She'd had to leave Wittenberg in January 1943, because she was not allowed to be in a relationship with a person of Jewish descent.

The Soviets were now in power, and he had the post of *Oberleiter*, senior leader, of the agricultural trade in the Wittenberg area, responsible for three companies. His work included visiting businesses by car and supervising the work of officers and administrators. Sophie was also able to travel with him now. The size of his own farm decreased, but they grew enough to feed the family. He was fairly well off, he said, except for a lack of coffee beans. He had obtained a pleasant flat as well, and had already bought furniture for it in the autumn of 1939. Their first child, Kaethe, was born in May 1946.

During the three years he spent in Wittenberg after the war, his responsibiliies increased to seven agricultural businesses in Sachsen-Anhalt, and he brought into productivity agricultural lands that had been laid waste in Klebitz and Destenberg. Later the farming business at Bösewig came under his charge. Between everything he was responsible for farming poultry, vegetable fields, orchards, horses and cattle.

His letters, however, could not reveal the family's intention to leave Wittenberg and the Soviet zone. On 7 July he wrote from Gehlenbeck, in the Lübbecke area to the west, in the British zone, and praised the order and cleanliness of British soldiers. But living conditions were very different. Things were in a state of chaos, and officers were corrupt. Goods were the means of exchange rather than money. A bottle of schnapps or 25 cigarettes would buy 20 litres of petrol. Bringing order to the community had been unsuccessful. There were no privileges for the Jews who had survived. Getting permission to leave the country was a matter of luck. Fritz's aim, however, was to obtain permission to move into that part of the country. The first condition was to have a flat in the British zone.

Although his work in the Russian zone was satisfying, people were under increasing pressure. The future seemed quite complicated. There was not much hope to be seen in the British zone. Jobs had already been divided among the former Nazis who had been 'de-Nazified' and the German refugees from the east, and no priority was given to half-Jews. Fritz asked Kate about agricultural conditions in England, and assumed, with his experience of farming and of looking after businesses, that he would be better off there. Nevertheless, he returned, for the time being, to Wittenberg.

Kate was now sending packets of delicacies to Fritz, including coffee and chocolate.

By October 1947, Fritz was back in Gehlenbeck with Sophie's sister, having had permission to travel. He went to the regional office's Exit and Entry branch to ask about the possibility of leaving the country and of obtaining permission to work in England. He was interested in farm machinery and asked Kate to send him leaflets on Ford's agricultural machines.

In less than a year his life changed dramatically as he took the daring decision to leave everything behind in Wittenberg. On 13 July Fritz wrote:

> I could not last any longer without getting involved in communist politics. I have therefore chosen to let go of matters slowly but safely. I have rented the clinic. I have put aside objects of personal value, clothes and the car. The things that we have are waiting for us in Berlin… If anyone wishes to set their sights towards the east, we can do nothing but recommend that they go there themselves. It is difficult to describe the conditions there. It wasn't easy to leave the fine work that I had there, but with the best will in the world it was not possible for me to stick at it. The most difficult question naturally, is what happens now. Things look quite meagre in terms of work as the flood of refugees is increasing. I therefore have to think about emigrating, as I do not have enough money to live on for months.

Fritz went to the military government in Lemgo, and made enquiries with the Manpower Division, German Movement Branch. He was told if someone could find work for him in England, made an application to the Ministry of Labour and arranged to pay for the journey, he could quickly have permission to travel to England, as farm workers were badly needed there. If they stayed in Wittenberg, Sophie might be considered to be a 'capitalist, Christian citizen of the Soviet zone, who has been exchanging letters with imperialist countries'.

Fritz described how he arranged his flight in a letter on 2 August 1949:

> We had been preparing to leave for months and had travelled regularly to Berlin and taken things there. In this way we could

take clothes, porcelain, money, pictures, files and other valuable things safely… If I had stayed to become a business leader of the state, the old farmers would have made the same accusation against me as we did against the Nazis… Among other things we were criticized for saying grace before food. As a business leader of the state I would have had to attend the SED [the Communist Party] school. Therefore the time came…

What will become of us? Other plans? The aim eventually: leave Germany.

In another letter within four weeks, on 27 August, he mentioned the possibility of emigrating to the USA or Australia, and he had already been in contact with the American consulate in Bremen.

This is the period during which Fritz started inventing agricultural machines. He wrote:

In the meantime I have developed a new kind of farm trailer and have connected the name Bosse with a vehicle company. The prototype will be built soon and it should be ready for the present exhibition.

He had another idea for model trains.

Kate made enquiries on his behalf in England and received a reply from the National Farmers' Union on 9 September saying that it would be necessary to find a farmer who would be willing to take Fritz, and he would have to make an application to the Ministry of Labour. It was clear that the process would not be easy. Work permission would be needed, and Fritz would also need a passport and visa, arranged in collaboration with the British Intelligence Authorities who would screen people for their politics. About the same time Fritz was told that an American church institution had started looking for work for him, and he also heard from Australia. He would have to spend two years working for someone else before being able to start up a business on his own.

Hierdurch erlaube ich mir, Sie höflichst darauf hinzuweisen, dass der **Mehrzweck-Muldenkippwagen** System Friedrich Bosse ein öl-hydraulisch betätigter Dreiseitenkippwagen, auf dem Stand **M 2 - 217** der 40. Wanderschau der D.L.G. in Frankfurt am Main (vom 11. 6. - 18. 6. 1950) ausgestellt ist. Darf ich mit Ihrem Besuch rechnen?

Mit vorzüglicher Hochachtung!

Gehlenbeck i. W., im Mai 1950

An advertisment for a waggon devised by Fritz

For the time being he had to be satisfied with living in Gehlenbeck, and he invited Kate and her family to spend a holiday in the home of his relatives. This took place, and I have a childhood memory of it: there was daily excitement anticipating the arrival of the ice cream van. We had an excursion to a nearby lake, into which I fell. I was not aware that we were with a family which was trying to bring order to their lives after the horrors and disruption of war.

Fritz settled in Lübbecke, and established a farm vehicle business. He died young, having turned 50 on 24 December 1965, when Gwyn and Kate were living for a few months in Egypt.

Kate

A SUBSTANTIAL PART OF THIS book has been Kate's story. In Rhondda she helped with youth activities and enjoyed the rich cultural life of the chapel. She was baptized in Moreia chapel, Pentre, by Gwyn's father, Robert Griffiths. Life in Bala was richer linguistically, and she became a part of the Welsh-speaking community. At the same time, hardly any contact was possible between Kate and her family throughout the war years. By October 1945, she had still not heard where her father was, and she sent letters to the foreign contacts of the Red Cross and St John's Order, without receiving a reply until 28 December 1945.

In Bala Kate supported German war prisoners who were in a nearby camp. She gave practical assistance through supplying essential food items and developed a friendship with some of the prisoners.

In a letter to Kate on 25 March 1947, Dolly wrote:

> A German war prisoner, who has been released, has told me that you are called the 'angel of Bala'. That's very good, Kathrinchen. This feeling of being responsible for many is surely one of the characteristics that have been inherited from Opa.

She developed her career as an author, and her works include *Anesmwyth Hoen* [Uneasy Vigour] (1941), *Fy Chwaer Efa a Storïau Eraill* [My Sister Eva and Other Stories] (1944), *Bwlch yn y Llen Haearn* [A Gap in the Iron Curtain] (1951), a volume which includes a banned documentary radio script which she wrote following an illegal journey to Germany after the war, and *Mae'r*

Galon wrth y Llyw [The Heart is at the Helm] (1957), a novel on the relationship between love and morality. Some of her stories were collected in the volume *Cariadau* [Loves] (1995). After she and Gwyn moved to Swansea she became responsible for the archaeological section of Swansea Museum, and she wrote scores of articles for the *South Wales Evening Post* on local history. She continued to write about literary matters to Welsh magazines, and published a volume on Russia and Berlin, *Taith i Rwsia a Berlin* [A Journey to Russia and Berlin] (1962), on modern and ancient Egypt, *Tywysennau o'r Aifft* [Ears of corn from Egypt] (1970) and on magic and medicine in *Byd y Dyn Hysbys* [World of the Folk Physician] (1977). A number of her articles were collected in *Teithiau'r Meddwl* [Journeys of the Mind] (2004).

She took an active part as well with national movements, especially Plaid Cymru (the Welsh National Party), arranging fundraising events and campaigning in elections. When Cymdeithas yr Iaith (The Welsh Language Society) was established in 1962, she supported it and was fined for refusing to pay for a parking ticket written in English. Her hospitality continued, and her home in Swansea became a social centre for Welsh literary figures and nationalists.

It could be said that the great work of her life did not start until she was 60 years old. In 1971 Gwyn had arranged that University College Wales, Swansea took possession of hundreds of objects from ancient Egypt that had not been unpacked since the 1930s. Kate worked assiduously on interpretation, arranging and cataloguing, and on the basis of her work the Egypt Museum was established on the university campus. She was curator of the collection until 1993. In 1998 the museum was opened in a new building, a few months after Kate had died on 4 April 1998, but she had lived to see work on these developments.

Kate working on objects from Ancient Egypt at Swansea University

The opening of the Egypt Museum

Descendents of Paul and Kaethe Bosse from Wales, with their families, in front of the old family home at 26 Heubnerstraße, Wittenberg, April 2010

Notes

Part 1: The Background

1   Wife of Pennar Davies, theologian, a friend of my father.

2   W. Marchewka, M. Schwibbe and A. Stephainski, *Journey in Time*, Medien, Göttingen, 2009.

3   Martin Luther, taken from J. Morgan Jones, *Traethodau'r Diwygiad* [Essays from the Revival], Hughes & Son, Wrexham, 1926, p. 59.

4   *Von den Juden und ihren Lügen*. The picture, and others, are taken from Ronny Kabus, *Jews of the Luthertown Wittenberg in the Third Reich*, State Center of Political Education Saxony-Anhalt, [n.d.].

5   Lewis Edwards in his translation tried to hide Faust's failure to find comfort in religion by a deliberate mistranslation. For 'Und leider auch Theologie' ['And also unfortunately theology'] Edwards translated 'Heblaw, ysywaeth duwinyddiaeth' ['Except, regrettably theology']. See H. Gruffudd, 'O Goethe i Gymru', *Taliesin*, 78–9, Rhagfyr 1992, pp. 121–32.

6   Günther Bosse, *Erinnerungen an meinen Vater-Bruchstücke*, family papers, 1996.

7   The description of the ceremony is found in Kate Bosse-Griffiths, *Teithiau'r Meddwl*, ed. J. Gwyn Griffiths, Y Lolfa, Talybont, 2004, p. 9.

8   Kate wrote a 120-page document about this journey, which is among the family papers.

Part 2: The Persecution

1   *Wittenberger Tageblatt*, 11 March 1933. Taken from Ronny Kabus, *Jews of the Luthertown Wittenberg in the Third Reich,* State Center of Political Education Saxony-Anhalt, [n.d.].

2   Much of the information that follows comes from Paul Bosse's document, '*Chronological description of the persecution of the family Bosse (and Maier) at Wittemberg/Luthertown by the NSAP and Gestapo during the years 1933/45 because of the marriage of Dr.Med. Paul Bosse (Aryan) to Kaethe Levin (Jewess) in 1906'*, 9 November 1945, family papers.

3   'Zeittafel zur Geschichte der Universität in Wittenberg': *www.hof.uni-halle.de*; accessed 2 February 2007; also 'Chronik der Lutherstadt Wittenberg': *http://underkunft.wittenberg.de*; accessed 2 February 2007.

4   Website *www.mdr.de*; accessed 2 February 2007.

5   Klinik Bosse, typewritten report, around 1981, 17pp., family papers.

6   A picture of the event appeared in the *Wittenberger Tageblatt*, 26 June 1935.

7   The story was related to me by Dr Senst, who was one of the children, January 2010.

8   *Lebenslauf*, 3 July 1946, family papers.

9   Landesarchiv Sachsen-Anhalt.

10 His career can be seen at *www.geocities.com/~orion47/WEHRMACHT/ HEER/Generalleutnant/BOROWIETZ*; accessed 9 May 2008.

11 Samuel W. Micham, *The Panzer Legions*, Stackpole Books, 2007, p. 125.

12 Suicide was the cause of his death, according to the online archive of the Deutsches Afrikakorps; accessed 19 September 2011.

13 The story was found in *usmbooks.com/borowietz.html*; accessed 9 May 2008.

14 The claim was that Herschel Grynszpan, a young German Jew, whose parents came from Poland, had shot a Nazi officer named Ernst vom Rath in Paris on 7 November 1938. The German retaliation came swiftly, with *Kristallnacht*.

15 These details are found in Kate Bosse-Griffiths, *Teithiau'r Meddwl*, ed. J. Gwyn Griffiths, Y Lolfa, Talybont, 2004, pp. 9–19.

16 Ibid.

17 Letter from D'Arcy W. Thompson, St Andrews, 15 September 1936.

18 Among the papers of Kate Bosse-Griffiths is material for a German publication on life in England (rather than Scotland), *This Country*, 52 pp.

19 Children in Germany receive presents on the feast of St Nicholas, 6 December.

20 'In the face of eternity.'

21 The second son of Dolly, daughter of Kaethe.

22 Hedwig Hache, the family's maid.

23 See Kate Bosse-Griffiths, *Teithiau'r Meddwl*, p. 19.

24 It is likely that Gwyn was staying at the time in the home of his sister Augusta – Ogi as she was known – as her husband Stephen had a teaching position there. They then moved to Glanrafon, near Bala, and had a quarter of a century of paradise.

25 This was a play presented in London's Shaftesbury Avenue, an adaptation of a novel by Jack Jones.

26 Gwyn here mentions an Egyptian engraved stone which Kate was studying.

27 Gwyn was preparing to address the Union of Baptists in Treharris.

Part 3: In the Grasp of War

1   Erika Viezens, *Aus ihrer Kindheit in Wittenberg, und Dessau, Dritter Reich bis DDR*. Family papers, [n.d.].

2   'J. Gwyn Griffiths yn ateb holiadur llenyddol Alun R. Jones', ['J. Gwyn Griffiths answering the literary questionnaire of Alun R. Jones'], *Yr Aradr*, the magazine of the Dafydd ap Gwilym Society, Oxford, No. 7, Christmas 1996, pp. 57–8.

3   Published by Weidenfeld & Nicolson, London, 2009.

4   See Martin Pabst, *Und Ihr wollt nichts gehört noch gesehen haben*, Taschenbuch, 2008.

5   Report by Fritz Bosse, '*Bericht über das Arbeitserziehunglager Zöschen*', unpublished, written at the end of 1945, family papers.

6   A king in Greek mythology who was forced to roll a stone up a hill, only for it to roll down again.

7   Taken from *Honoring American Liberators*, United States Holocaust Memorial, p. 3. The picture is taken from this document.

8   I had the story orally from Günther.

9   Notes I had from Ulrich, 3 August 2010.

10   'J. Gwyn Griffiths yn ateb holiadur llenyddol Alun R. Jones', *Yr Aradr*, No. 7, 1996, p. 52.

11   See articles by Llinos Angharad, 'Cylch Cadwgan', *Barn*, 312, January 1989, pp. 32–4, and *Barn*, 313, February 1989, pp. 30–1.

12   These were published in *Seren Cymru* (not *Seren Gomer* as noted in J. E. Caerwyn Williams ed., *Ysgrifau Beirniadol XXV*, Gwasg Gee, 1999, p. 108) during 1940–2.

13   See Nia Mai Williams, 'Cynnyrch aelodau Cylch Cadwgan a ymddangosodd mewn detholiad o gylchgronau rhwng 1935 ac 1945', ['The works of members of Cylch Cadwgan which appeared in a selection of magazines between 1935 and 1945'], *Ysgrifau Beirniadol XXV*, pp. 105–111.

14   Gruffydd Davies, 'Sais yn ymosod ar Hywel Harris' ['An Englishman attacking Hywel Harris'], *Heddiw* [Today], vol. 6, no. 2, July 1940, pp. 43–7.

15   Christopher Davies, Swansea, 1972. There is a discussion on the two novels by Nia Mai Williams, 'Nofelau am gylch Cadwgan gan ddau aelod' ['Novels on Cylch Cadwgan by two members'] in *Ysgrifau Beirniadol XXV*, p.p. 86–111.

16   Llyfrau'r Dryw, Llandybïe, 1968.

17   'J. Gwyn Griffiths yn ateb holiadur llenyddol Alun R. Jones', *Yr Aradr*, No. 7, 1996, p. 58.

18   The winning Eisteddfod poem 'Atgof' [Recollection] by Prosser Rhys was
      daring in its day for suggesting a physical relationship between two men.

19   There is some discussion on the novel in an M.A. dissertation by Bethan
      Eleri Hicks, *Astudiaeth o Yrfa Lenyddol Kate Bosse-Griffiths* ['A Study of
      the Literary Career of Kate Bosse-Griffiths'], University of Wales Swansea,
      2001. See also Nia Mai Williams, *'Cylch Cadwgan'*, M.A. dissertation,
      University of Wales Bangor, 1994.

20   Densil Morgan mentions the courtship between Pennar Davies and the
      'Grey Lizard', an Indian girl from Mexico, in *Pennar Davies*, University of
      Wales Press, Cardiff, 2003, p.p. 28–9.

21   'I believe because there is no means of expressing it.'

22   *Cyfansoddiadau a Beirniadaethau* [Compositions and Adjudications],
      Eisteddfod Genedlaethol 1942, p. 144.

23   *Fy Chwaer Efa*, Llyfrau Pawb, Gwasg Gee, Dinbych, 1944.

24   It is possible that this letter is the source of incorrect information regarding
      the fate of both as noted in Densil Morgan's book, *Pennar Davies*, University
      of Wales Press, Cardiff, 2003, p. 69.

25   A collection of his pictures and posters can be seen in John Willet, *Heartfield
      versus Hitler*, Hazan, Paris, 1997.

26   Inge Scholl, *Die Weisse Rose*, Fischer Taschenbuch Verlag, Frankfurt, 1982;
      10th impression, May 2003.

27   Ibid., p. 12.

28   Photostat copies are available in *Austellung Widerstand gegen den
      Nationalsozialismus, resources file in Gedenkstätte Deutscher Widerstand*.

29   Ein Gespräch mit Jürgen Wittenstein: 'Einer mußte es doch machen',
      website *haGalil.com*; accessed 22 March 2011. There is a conversation here
      with J.W., who was one of the members of Weiße Rose.

30   Inge Scholl, *Die Weisse Rose*, pp. 88–9. The translation is taken from http://
      dieweisserose.weebly.com/the-fourth-leaflet.html, accessed 3-1-2014.

31   Ibid., p. 93.

32   This evidence is given by Jürgen Wittenstein, see above.

33   *Sechstes Flugblat der Weißen Rose, Februar 1943*, from the collection *Austellung
      Widerstand gegen den Nationalsozialismus*, Section 16.9 F.

34   Birgit Gewehr, *Hamburger Abendblatt*, obtained from the website *Stolpersteine
      in Hamburg*; accessed 23 March 2011.

35   Part of the story was taken from Christiane Benzenberg, 'Denkmäler für
      die Widerstandsgruppe, "Weiße Rose" in München und Hamburg', M.A.
      dissertation, Bonn University, 1993.

36   Information from the website *Gymnasium-ohmoor.de*; accessed 23 March
      2011.

37   These quotations were obtained from Birgit Gewehr, see above.

38   The website *Gymnasium-ohmoor.de* says that there is no certainty whether he was hanged or shot, and this could have occurred between 20 and 23 April 1945.

39   I had a conversation with him in January 2010.

40   These facts were obtained from Ute Stummeyer, Dolly's daughter, in family papers, and conveyed to me in a letter, 22 July 2010.

41   Claus Füllberg-Stolberg and others, *Frauen in Konzentrationslagern*, Edition Temmen, Bremen, 1994, p. 13.

42   Ibid., p. 15.

43   *Michelangelo in Ravensbrück,* Da Capo Press, 2006, pp. 262–3.

44   Taken from Claus Füllberg-Stolberg and others, *Frauen in Konzentrationslagern*, p. 17.

45   Jack G. Morrison, *Ravensbrück*, Markus Wiener Publications, Princeton, 2000, pp. 276–7.

46   Ibid., pp. 278–81.

47   Taken from Claus Füllberg-Stolberg and others, *Frauen in Konzentrationslagern*, p. 22.

48   Ibid., p. 21.

49   Ibid., p. 24.

Part 4: After the War

1   The clinic's history is available in *Chronik der Klinik Bosse Wittenberg,* Nicolaus Särchen, K Jonas and Torsten Sielaff, Wittenberg, 2009.

2   The details were recorded by me after a conversation with my cousin, Ute, Dolly's daughter, between 2 and 4 May 1998.